The **McGraw·Hill** *Companies*

Kindergarten

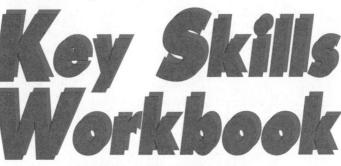

Math • Thinking Skills
Reading • Phonics

A McGraw·Hill/Warner Bros. Workbook

Giant

Table of Contents

Credits:
McGraw-Hill Learning Materials Editorial/Production Team
Vincent F. Douglas, B.S. and M. Ed.
Tracy R. Paulus
Jennifer P. Blashkiw

Design Studio
Mike Legendre; Creativity On Demand

Warner Bros. Worldwide Publishing Editorial/Production Team
Michael Harkavy   Charles Carney
Paula Allen   Allen Helbig
Victoria Selover

Illustrators
Cover: Animated Arts!™
Interior: Arkadia Illustration & Design — London; Renegade Animation, Inc.

McGraw-Hill
Consumer Products

A Division of The McGraw·Hill Companies

Send all inquiries to:
McGraw-Hill Consumer Products
250 Old Wilson Bridge Road
Worthington, Ohio 43085

1-57768-240-8

The McGraw·Hill Companies

Kindergarten

Vowels & Consonants • Beginning Sounds
Capital & Lowercase Letters

A McGraw·Hill/Warner Bros. Workbook

Table of Contents

Table of Contents (continued)

A a

apple

Directions: Have your child look at the picture in the first row and say *apple* while listening for the short a sound. Ask your child to name the pictures, then circle those that begin with the same short a sound as the first picture. Your child should trace and write Aa in the space provided. **Skill:** Identifying the short a vowel sound.

CONSONANTS: B

Bugs's bomb

6

Directions: Have your child look at the picture in the first row and say *Bugs's bomb* while listening for the beginning b sound. Ask your child to name the pictures, then circle those that begin with the same b sound as the first picture. Your child should trace and write Bb in the space provided. ***Skill:*** Identifying the beginning sound b.

MATCHING LETTERS

C c

Claude's collar

D d

Daffy's dishes

C	C	G	C	O
c	o	c	n	c
D	O	D	D	B
d	d	h	g	d

 7

Directions: Have your child look at the pictures and say the words at the top of the page. In each row, ask your child to circle the letters that are the same as the first letter in the row. **Skill:** Identifying capital and lowercase Cc and Dd.

CONSONANTS: C

Cc

Coyote's cannon

Directions: Have your child look at the picture in the first row and say *Coyote's cannon* while listening for the beginning c sound. Ask your child to name the pictures, then circle those that begin with the same c sound as the first picture. Your child should trace and write Cc in the space provided. **Skill:** Identifying the beginning sound c.

CONSONANTS: D

Daffy's drum

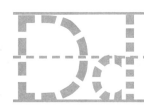

Directions: Have your child look at the picture in the first row and say *Daffy's drum* while listening for the beginning d sound. Ask your child to name the pictures, then circle those that begin with the same d sound as the first picture. Your child should trace and write Dd in the space provided. **Skill:** Identifying the beginning sound d.

MATCHING LETTERS

Ee	 Eggbert's **e**gg	Ff	 Foghorn's **f**ootball

E	(E)	F	B	E
e	a	e	v	e
F	T	E	F	F
f	f	l	f	h

Directions: Have your child look at the pictures and say the words at the top of the page. In each row, ask your child to circle the letters that are the same as the first letter in the row. **Skill:** Identifying capital and lowercase Ee and Ff.

VOWELS: SHORT E

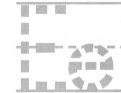

Elmer's elbow

Directions: Have your child look at the picture in the first row and say *Elmer's elbow* while listening for the short e sound. Ask your child to name the pictures, then circle those that begin with the same short e sound as the first picture. Your child should trace and write Ee in the space provided. ***Skill:*** Identifying the short e vowel sound.

11

REVIEW

a and e

apple

egg

Directions: Have your child name the picture at the beginning of each row. Then ask your child to circle each picture in the row whose name begins with the same sound as the first picture. **Skill:** Identifying the short a and e vowel sounds.

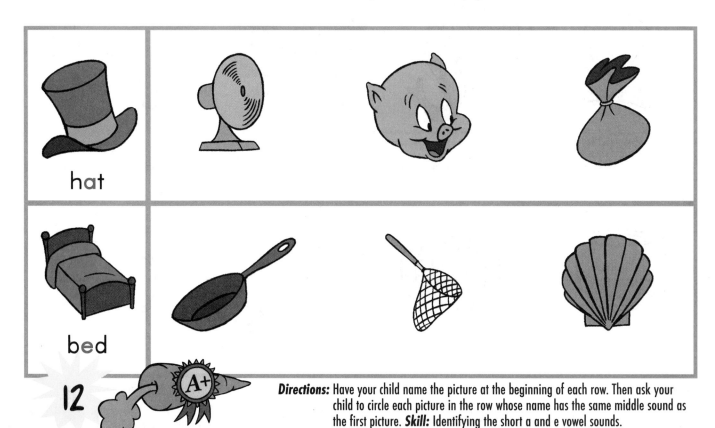

hat

bed

12

Directions: Have your child name the picture at the beginning of each row. Then ask your child to circle each picture in the row whose name has the same middle sound as the first picture. **Skill:** Identifying the short a and e vowel sounds.

CONSONANTS: F

Foghorn's fan

Directions: Have your child look at the picture in the first row and say *Foghorn's fan* while listening for the beginning f sound. Ask your child to name the pictures, then circle those that begin with the same f sound as the first picture. Your child should trace and write Ff in the space provided. **Skill:** Identifying the beginning sound f.

13

b, c, d, f

REVIEW

Bugs

Claude

Daffy

Foghorn

Directions: Have your child say the letter and name the character at the beginning of each row. Then ask your child to circle each picture in the row whose name begins with the sound made by that letter. **Skill:** Identifying the beginning sounds b, c, d and f.

CONSONANTS: G

Granny's gift

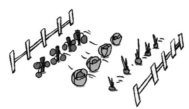

Directions: Have your child look at the picture in the first row and say *Granny's gift* while listening for the beginning g sound. Ask your child to name the pictures, then circle those that begin with the same g sound as the first picture. Your child should trace and write Gg in the space provided. *Skill:* Identifying the beginning sound g.

NAME

CONSONANTS: H

Hubie's hat

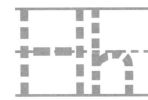

16

Directions: Have your child look at the picture in the first row and say *Hubie's hat* while listening for the beginning h sound. Ask your child to name the pictures, then circle those that begin with the same h sound as the first picture. Your child should trace and write Hh in the space provided. *Skill:* Identifying the beginning sound h.

MATCHING LETTERS

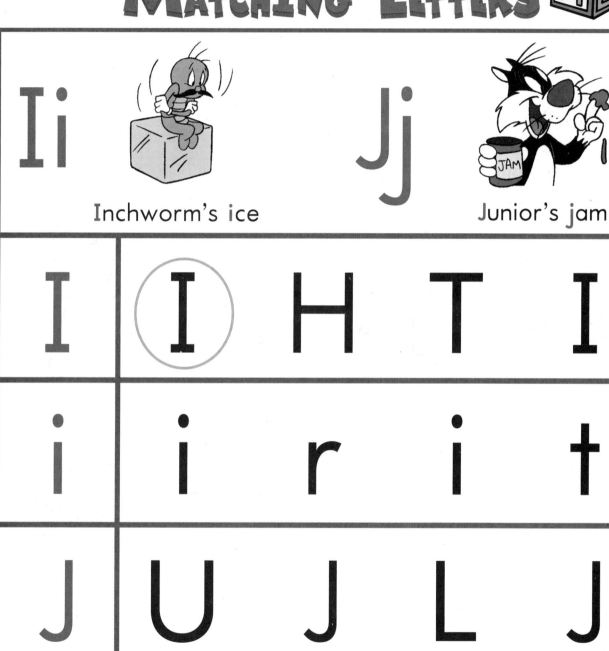

Ii	Inchworm's ice	Jj	Junior's jam

I	I	H	T	I
i	i	r	i	t
J	U	J	L	J
j	j	p	j	q

Directions: Have your child look at the pictures and say the words at the top of the page. In each row, ask your child to circle the letters that are the same as the first letter in the row. **Skill:** Identifying capital and lowercase Ii and Jj.

VOWELS: SHORT I

Inchworm's ink

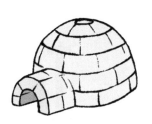   

   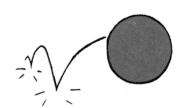

Directions: Have your child look at the picture in the first row and say *Inchworm's ink* while listening for the short i sound. Ask your child to name the pictures, then circle those that begin with the same short i sound as the first picture. Your child should trace and write Ii in the space provided. **Skill:** Identifying the short i vowel sound.

CONSONANTS: Jj

Junior's jacks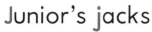

Directions: Have your child look at the picture in the first row and say *Junior's jacks* while listening for the beginning j sound. Ask your child to name the pictures, then circle those that begin with the same j sound as the first picture. Your child should trace and write Jj in the space provided. *Skill:* Identifying the beginning sound j.

MATCHING LETTERS

K k		L l	
	K-9's kite		Lion's lock

K	K	N	R	K

k	k	l	k	t

L	J	L	I	L

l	b	l	l	d

Directions: Have your child look at the pictures and say the words at the top of the page. In each row, ask your child to circle the letters that are the same as the first letter in the row. **Skill:** Identifying capital and lowercase Kk and Ll.

CONSONANTS: K

Kitten's kiss

Directions: Have your child look at the picture in the first row and say *Kitten's kiss* while listening for the beginning k sound. Ask your child to name the pictures, then circle those that begin with the same k sound as the first picture. Your child should trace and write Kk in the space provided. *Skill:* Identifying the beginning sound k.

N**AME** _____

R**EVIEW**

 Granny	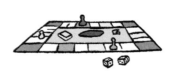  
 Hubie	  
 Junior	  
 K-9	  

22

Directions: Have your child say the letter and name the character at the beginning of each row. Then ask your child to circle each picture in the row whose name begins with the sound made by that letter. *Skill:* Identifying the beginning sounds g, h, j and k.

CONSONANTS: L

Lola's lamb

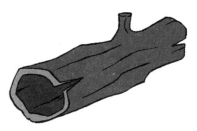

Directions: Have your child look at the picture in the first row and say *Lola's lamb* while listening for the beginning *l* sound. Ask your child to name the pictures, then write *l* under each picture that begins with the same sound as the first picture. Your child should trace and write Ll in the space provided. **Skill:** Identifying the beginning sound l.

MATCHING LETTERS

M m		N n	
	Marvin's money		Nasty's nickel

M	n	(m)	r	m
m	M	K	M	N
N	n	m	n	h
n	Y	N	W	N

24

Directions: Have your child look at the pictures and say the words at the top of the page. In each row, ask your child to circle the letters that belong with the first letter in the row. **Skill:** Identifying capital and lowercase Mm and Nn.

CONSONANTS: M

Martian mail

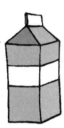

Directions: Have your child look at the picture in the first row and say *Martian mail* while listening for the beginning m sound. Ask your child to name the pictures, then circle those that begin with the same m sound as the first picture. Your child should trace and write Mm in the space provided. **Skill:** Identifying the beginning sound m.

25

CONSONANTS: N

Nn

Nelly's neck

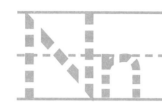

Directions: Have your child look at the picture in the first row and say *Nelly's neck* while listening for the beginning n sound. Ask your child to name the pictures, then circle those that begin with the same n sound as the first picture. Your child should trace and write Nn in the space provided. **Skill:** Identifying the beginning sound n.

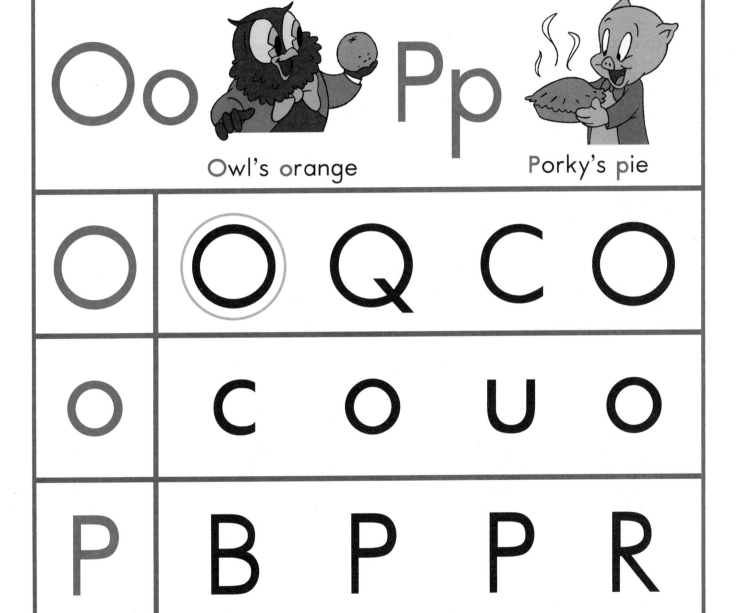

Oo — Owl's orange

Pp — Porky's pie

O	O	Q	C	O
o	C	O	U	O
P	B	P	P	R
p	p	q	p	j

Directions: Have your child look at the pictures and say the words at the top of the page. In each row, ask your child to circle the letters that are the same as the first letter in the row. **Skill:** Identifying capital and lowercase Oo and Pp.

27

VOWELS: SHORT O

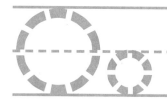

Oliver's oven

Directions: Have your child look at the picture in the first row and say *Oliver's oven* while listening for the beginning o sound. Ask your child to name the pictures, then circle those that begin with the same o sound as the first picture. Your child should trace and write Oo in the space provided. **Skill:** Identifying the short o vowel sound.

REVIEW

igloo

octopus

Directions: Have your child name the picture at the beginning of each row. Then ask your
child to circle each picture in the row whose name begins with the same sound as
the first picture. **Skill:** Identifying the short i and o vowel sounds.

pig

mop

Directions: Have your child name the picture at the beginning of each row. Then ask your
child to circle each picture in the row whose name has the same middle sound as
the first picture. **Skill:** Identifying the short i and o vowel sounds.

NAME _____

CONSONANTS: P

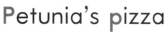

Petunia's pizza

30

Directions: Have your child look at the picture in the first row and say *Petunia's pizza* while listening for the beginning p sound. Ask your child to name the pictures, then circle those that begin with the same p sound as the first picture. Your child should trace and write Pp in the space provided. ***Skill:*** Identifying the beginning sound p.

REVIEW

 Lola		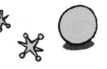
 Marvin	 	 
 Nero		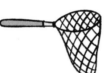 
 Porky		 

Directions: Have your child say the letter and name the character at the beginning of each row. Then ask your child to circle each picture in the row whose name begins with the sound made by that letter. **Skill:** Identifying the beginning sounds l, m, n and p.

MATCHING LETTERS

Qq Rr

Quentin Quail's
quiet

Road Runner
runs

| Q | e | q | q | d |

| q | Q | O | U | Q |

| R | r | n | m | r |

| r | P | R | B | R |

Directions: Have your child look at the pictures and say the words at the top of the page. In each row, ask your child to circle the letters that belong with the first letter in the row. **Skill:** Identifying capital and lowercase Qq and Rr.

CONSONANTS: Q

Quentin's quilt

   **QUACK!**

 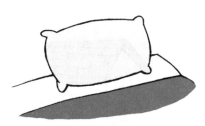  

Directions: Have your child look at the picture in the first row and say *Quentin's quilt* while listening for the beginning q sound. Ask your child to name the pictures, then circle those that begin with the same q sound as the first picture. Your child should trace and write Qq in the space provided. **Skill:** Identifying the beginning sound q.

CONSONANTS: R

Free Roses
for Road
Runners

R r - - - - - - - - - - - - - - - - -

Road Runner's
rose

34

Directions: Have your child look at the picture in the first row and say *Road Runner's rose* while listening for the beginning r sound. Ask your child to name the pictures, then circle those that begin with the same r sound as the first picture. Your child should trace and write Rr in the space provided. *Skill:* Identifying the beginning sound r.

MATCHING LETTERS

Ss Speedy sings	Tt Tweety talks

S	S c s o
s	G S C S
T	l t t i
t	T Y T X

Directions: Have your child look at the pictures and say the words at the top of the page. In each row, ask your child to circle the letters that belong with the first letter in the row. **Skill:** Identifying capital and lowercase Ss and Tt.

35

CONSONANTS: S

Sylvester stands

 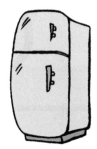  

Directions: Have your child look at the picture in the first row and say *Sylvester stands* while listening for the beginning s sound. Ask your child to name the pictures, then circle those that begin with the same s sound as the first picture. Your child should trace and write Ss in the space provided. **Skill:** Identifying the beginning sound s.

CONSONANTS: T

Tweety's train

Directions: Have your child look at the picture in the first row and say *Tweety's train* while listening for the beginning t sound. Ask your child to name the pictures, then circle those that begin with the same t sound as the first picture. Your child should trace and write Tt in the space provided. ***Skill:*** Identifying the beginning sound t.

Name _____

q, r, s, t

REVIEW

 Quentin	 QUACK!		
 Ralph			
 Sam			
 Tweety			

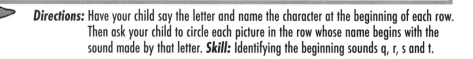

Directions: Have your child say the letter and name the character at the beginning of each row. Then ask your child to circle each picture in the row whose name begins with the sound made by that letter. **Skill:** Identifying the beginning sounds q, r, s and t.

MATCHING LETTERS

U	u
Ugly underwear	

V	v
Vulture's valentine	

U	v u n u

u	U O U C

V	W V U V

v	V N Y V

Directions: Have your child look at the pictures and say the words at the top of the page. In each row, ask your child to circle the letters that belong with the first letter in the row. **Skill:** Identifying capital and lowercase Uu and Vv.

VOWELS: SHORT U

Umpire Fudd

40

Directions: Have your child look at the picture in the first row and say *Umpire Fudd* while listening for the short u sound. Ask your child to name the pictures, then circle those that begin with the same short u sound as the first picture. Your child should trace and write Uu in the space provided. ***Skill:*** Identifying the short u vowel sound.

CONSONANTS: V

Vulture's vest

Directions: Have your child look at the picture in the first row and say *Vulture's vest* while listening for the beginning v sound. Ask your child to name the pictures, then circle those that begin with the same v sound as the first picture. Your child should trace and write Vv in the space provided. ***Skill:*** Identifying the beginning sound v.

MATCHING LETTERS

W w  X x

wet Witch   Fox's box

W	N	W	Y	W

W	W	V	X	W

X	Z	X	X	Y

x	x	y	x	t

Directions: Have your child look at the pictures and say the words at the top of the page. In each row, ask your child to circle the letters that are the same as the first letter in the row. **Skill:** Identifying capital and lowercase Ww and Xx.

CONSONANTS: W

Witch's wedding

Directions: Have your child look at the picture in the first row and say *Witch's wedding* while listening for the beginning w sound. Ask your child to name the pictures, then circle those that begin with the same w sound as the first picture. Your child should trace and write Ww in the space provided. *Skill:* Identifying the beginning sound w.

 43

CONSONANTS: X

Fox's mix

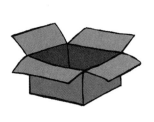   

Directions: Have your child look at the picture in the first row and say *Fox's mix* while listening for the final x sound. Ask your child to name the pictures, then circle those that end with the same x sound as the first picture. Your child should trace and write Xx in the space provided. **Skill:** Identifying the final sound x.

CONSONANTS: Y

Yosemite yells

45

Directions: Have your child look at the picture in the first row and say *Yosemite yells* while listening for the beginning y sound. Ask your child to name the pictures, then circle those that begin with the same y sound as the first picture. Your child should trace and write Yy in the space provided. ***Skill:*** Identifying the beginning sound y.

ZIP

CONSONANTS: Z

Zebra's zipper

Directions: Have your child look at the picture in the first row and say *Zebra's zipper* while listening for the beginning z sound. Ask your child to name the pictures, then circle those that begin with the same z sound as the first picture. Your child should trace and write Zz in the space provided. **Skill:** Identifying the beginning sound z.

NAME

REVIEW

v, w, x, y, z

 Vulture			
 Wile E.			
 Fox			
Yosemite Sam			
 Taz			

Directions: Have your child say the letter and name the character at the beginning of each row. Then ask your child to circle each picture in the row whose name has the sound made by that letter. **Skill:** Identifying the beginning sounds v, w, y and z; the final sound x.

47

VOWELS: LONG A

ā

ape

Directions: Have your child look at the picture at the top of the page and say the word *ape* while listening for the long a vowel sound. Ask your child to name the other pictures, then circle those with the same long a sound.
Skill: Identifying the long a vowel sound.

VOWELS: LONG A

ā  cake

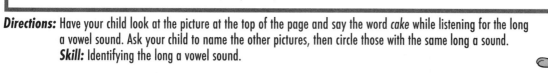

Directions: Have your child look at the picture at the top of the page and say the word *cake* while listening for the long
a vowel sound. Ask your child to name the other pictures, then circle those with the same long a sound.
Skill: Identifying the long a vowel sound.

VOWELS: LONG A

$\overline{a}$ ape

man   mane

cape   cap

tap   tape

plan   plane

hate   hat

pane   pan

50

Directions: Have your child look at the picture at the top of the page and say the word *ape* while listening for the long a vowel sound. Ask your child to name the other pictures. Ask your child to circle, then write the words for those pictures with the same long a sound. *Skill:* Identifying the long a vowel sound.

VOWELS: LONG A

ai  jail

Directions: Have your child look at the picture at the top of the page and say the word *jail* while listening for the long
a vowel sound. Ask your child to name the other pictures, then circle those with the same long a sound.
Skill: Identifying the long a vowel sound.

Vowels: Long A

ai  nail

m l r g s l

  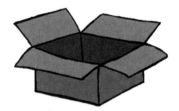

p l t l b x

Directions: Have your child look at the picture at the top of the page and say the word *nail* while listening for the long a vowel sound. Ask your child to name the other pictures, then write ai if the words have the same long a sound.
Skill: Identifying the long a vowel sound.

VOWELS: LONG I

 ī      ice

 53

Directions: Have your child look at the picture at the top of the page and say the word *ice* while listening for the long i vowel sound. Ask your child to name the other pictures, then circle those with the same long i sound.
Skill: Identifying the long i vowel sound.

NAME

VOWELS: LONG I

ī  hive

54

Directions: Have your child look at the picture at the top of the page and say the word *hive* while listening for the long i vowel sound. Ask your child to name the other pictures, then circle those with the same long i sound. **Skill:** Identifying the long i vowel sound.

VOWELS: LONG I

ī  tiger

5  6

f v   s x   d c

k t   b k   s f

Directions: Have your child look at the picture at the top of the page and say the word *tiger* while listening for the long i vowel sound. Ask your child to name the other pictures, then write i-e if the words have the same long i sound. **Skill:** Identifying the long i vowel sound.

55

VOWELS: LONG I

w _i pe

b _i te

t _i me

Directions: Have your child say the sound of each letter while tracing the line. Then have your child write the words in the space provided. **Skill:** Identifying the long i vowel sound.

VOWELS: LONG O

oa  soap

57

Directions: Have your child look at the picture at the top of the page and say the word *soap* while listening for the long o vowel sound. Ask your child to name the other pictures, then circle those with the same long o sound.
Skill: Identifying the long o vowel sound.

VOWELS: LONG O

oa  toast

Directions: Have your child look at the picture at the top of the page and say the word *toast* while listening for the long o vowel sound. Ask your child to name the other pictures, then circle those with the same long o sound.
Skill: Identifying the long o vowel sound.

VOWELS: LONG O

oa  coach

f l ____ t

n ____ l

r ____ d

b ____ t

b ____ k

t ____ st

Directions: Have your child look at the picture at the top of the page and say the word *coach* while listening for the long o vowel sound. Ask your child to name the other pictures, then write *oa* if the words have the same long o sound. **Skill:** Identifying the long o vowel sound.

VOWELS: LONG O

$\bar{o}$

crow

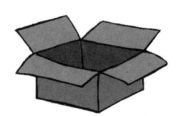

Directions: Have your child look at the picture at the top of the page and say the word *crow* while listening for the long o vowel sound. Ask your child to name the other pictures, then circle those with the same long o sound.
Skill: Identifying the long o vowel sound.

VOWELS: LONG E

ea   Eager Beaver

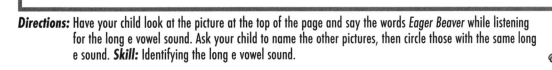

Directions: Have your child look at the picture at the top of the page and say the words *Eager Beaver* while listening for the long e vowel sound. Ask your child to name the other pictures, then circle those with the same long e sound. **Skill:** Identifying the long e vowel sound.

VOWELS: LONG E

ea   eagle

s l   t m   g t

l f   b k   n l

Directions: Have your child look at the picture at the top of the page and say the word *eagle* while listening for the long e vowel sound. Ask your child to name the other pictures, then write ea if the words have the same long e sound. *Skill:* Identifying the long e vowel sound.

VOWELS: LONG E

ee  sleepy Tweety

Directions: Have your child look at the picture at the top of the page and say the words *sleepy Tweety* while listening for the long e vowel sound. Ask your child to name the other pictures, then circle those with the same long e sound. **Skill:** Identifying the long e vowel sound.

VOWELS: LONG E

ee  Sheepdog sees

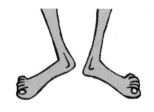

f t b

qu n

sh p d

r r d

Directions: Have your child look at the picture at the top of the page and say the words *Sheepdog sees* while listening for the long e vowel sound. Ask your child to name the other pictures, then write ee if the words have the same long e sound. **Skill:** Identifying the long e vowel sound.

VOWELS: LONG U

ū  puma

Directions: Have your child look at the picture at the top of the page and say the word *puma* while listening for the long u vowel sound. Ask your child to name the other pictures, then circle those with the same long u sound. **Skill:** Identifying the long u vowel sound.

VOWELS: LONG U

ū  Hubie's suitcase

t b

b n

t n

m l

c p

J n

66

Directions: Have your child look at the picture at the top of the page and say the words *Hubie's suitcase* while listening for the long u vowel sound. Ask your child to name the other pictures, then write u-e if the words have the same long u sound. **Skill:** Identifying the long u vowel sound.

ANSWER KEY

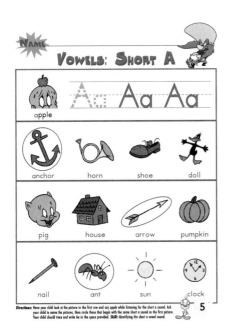

VOWELS: SHORT A

apple

Aa Aa Aa

anchor · horn · shoe · doll

pig · house · arrow · pumpkin

nail · ant · sun · clock

Directions: Have your child look at the picture in the first row and say apple while listening for the short a sound. Ask your child to name the pictures, then circle those that begin with the same short a sound as the first picture. Your child should trace and write Aa in the space provided. Skill: Identifying the short a vowel sound.

5

CONSONANTS: B

Bugs's bomb

Bb Bb Bb

cow · block · bed · popcorn

pizza · bone · tree · bird

boat · rope · bath tub · book

6

Directions: Have your child look at the picture in the first row and say Bugs's bomb while listening for the beginning b sound. Ask your child to name the pictures, then circle those that begin with the same b sound as the first picture. Your child should trace and write Bb in the space provided. Skill: Identifying the beginning sound b.

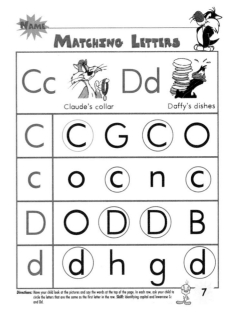

MATCHING LETTERS

Cc · Dd

Claude's collar · Daffy's dishes

C	C	G	C	O
c	o	c	n	c
D	O	D	D	B
d	d	h	g	d

Directions: Have your child look at the pictures and say the words at the top of the page. In each row, ask your child to circle the letters that are the same as the first letter in the row. Skill: Identifying capital and lowercase Cc and Dd.

7

CONSONANTS: C

Coyote's cannon

Cc Cc Cc

cap · toast · clock · comb

cake · balloon · carrot · candle

bee · can · cookie · cow

8

Directions: Have your child look at the picture in the first row and say Coyote's cannon while listening for the beginning c sound. Ask your child to name the pictures, then circle those that begin with the same c sound as the first picture. Your child should trace and write Cc in the space provided. Skill: Identifying the beginning sound c.

CONSONANTS: D

Daffy's drum

Dd Dd Dd

door · camera · dime · dominoes

balloon · dog · dishes · desk

dinosaur · boat · doll · bone

Directions: Have your child look at the picture in the first row and say Daffy's drum while listening for the beginning d sound. Ask your child to name the pictures, then circle those that begin with the same d sound as the first picture. Your child should trace and write Dd in the space provided. Skill: Identifying the beginning sound d.

9

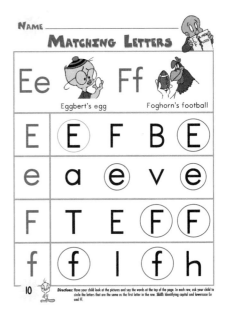

MATCHING LETTERS

Ee · Ff

Eggbert's egg · Foghorn's football

E	E	F	B	E
e	a	e	v	e
F	T	E	F	F
f	f	l	f	h

10

Directions: Have your child look at the pictures and say the words at the top of the page. In each row, ask your child to circle the letters that are the same as the first letter in the row. Skill: Identifying capital and lowercase Ee and Ff.

67

ANSWER KEY

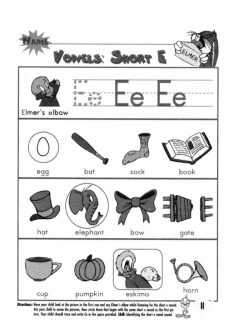

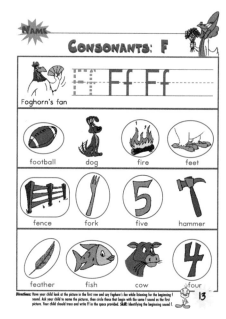

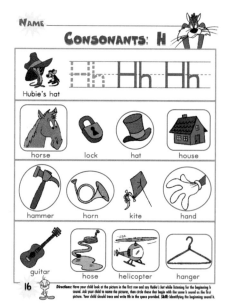

ANSWER KEY

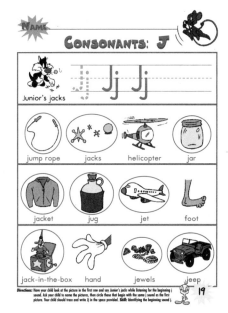

ANSWER KEY

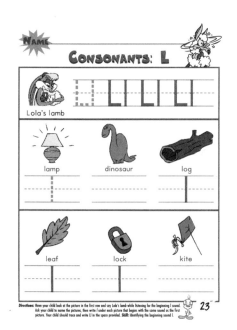

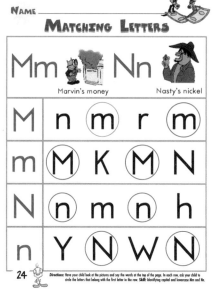

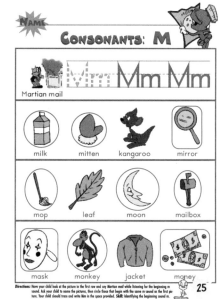

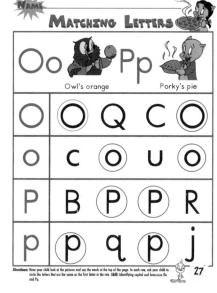

ANSWER KEY

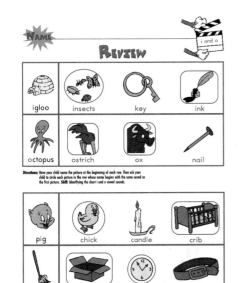

REVIEW

igloo	insects	key	ink
octopus	ostrich	ox	nail

Directions: Have your child name the picture at the beginning of each row. Then ask your child to circle each picture in the row whose name begins with the same sound as the first picture. **Skill:** Identifying the short i and o vowel sounds.

pig	chick	candle	crib
mop	box	clock	belt

Directions: Have your child name the picture at the beginning of each row. Then ask your child to circle each picture in the row whose name has the same middle sound as the first picture. **Skill:** Identifying the short i and o vowel sounds. **29**

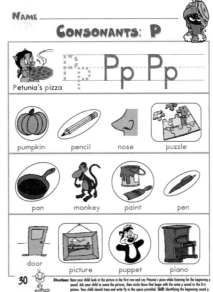

CONSONANTS: P

Petunia's pizza — Pp Pp Pp

pumpkin	pencil	nose	puzzle
pan	monkey	paint	pen
door	picture	puppet	piano

30 Directions: Have your child look at the picture in the first row and say Petunia's pizza while listening for the beginning p sound. Ask your child to name the pictures, then circle those that begin with the same p sound as the first picture. Your child should trace and write Pp in the space provided. **Skill:** Identifying the beginning sound p.

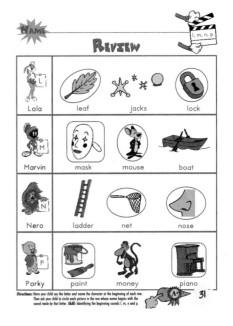

REVIEW

L Lola	leaf	jacks	lock
M Marvin	mask	mouse	boat
N Nero	ladder	net	nose
P Porky	paint	money	piano

Directions: Have your child say the letter and name the character at the beginning of each row. Then ask your child to circle each picture in the row whose name begins with the sound made by that letter. **Skill:** Identifying the beginning sounds l, m, n and p. **31**

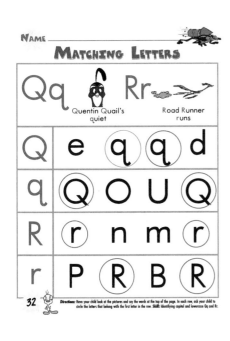

MATCHING LETTERS

Qq Quentin Quail's quiet   Rr Road Runner runs

Q	e	q	q	d
q	Q	O	U	Q
R	r	n	m	r
r	P	R	B	R

32 Directions: Have your child look at the pictures and say the words at the top of the page. In each row, ask your child to circle the letters that belong with the first letter in the row. **Skill:** Identifying capital and lowercase Qq and Rr.

CONSONANTS: Q

Quentin's quilt — Qq Qq Qq

queen	bow	needle	quack
log	question mark	pencil	lamp
octopus	pillow	quarter	monkey

Directions: Have your child look at the picture in the first row and say Quentin's quilt while listening for the beginning q sound. Ask your child to name the pictures, then circle those that begin with the same q sound as the first picture. Your child should trace and write Qq in the space provided. **Skill:** Identifying the beginning sound q. **33**

CONSONANTS: R

Road Runner's rose — Rr Rr Rr

rooster	Fox	question mark	rain
ring	mailbox	rainbow	rake
pot	ruler	roof	rattle

34 Directions: Have your child look at the picture in the first row and say Road Runner's rose while listening for the beginning r sound. Ask your child to name the pictures, then circle those that begin with the same r sound as the first picture. Your child should trace and write Rr in the space provided. **Skill:** Identifying the beginning sound r.

ANSWER KEY

MATCHING LETTERS

Ss — Speedy sings
Tt — Tweety talks

S	S	C	S	O
S	G	S	C	S
T	I	T	T	i
t	T	Y	T	X

Directions: Have your child look at the pictures and say the words at the top of the page. In each row, ask your child to circle the letters that belong with the first letter in the row. Skill: Identifying capital and lowercase Ss and Tt.

35

CONSONANTS: S

Sylvester stands — Ss Ss

sun	soap	moon	sock
scissors	refrigerator	sink	saw
six	sandwich	saddle	needle

36

Directions: Have your child look at the picture in the first row and say Sylvester stands while listening for the beginning s sound. Ask your child to name the pictures, then circle those that begin with the same s sound as the first picture. Your child should trace and write Ss in the space provided. Skill: Identifying the beginning sound s.

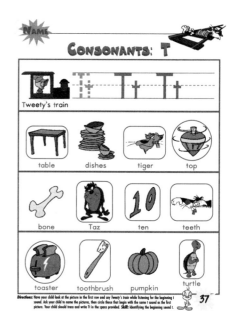

CONSONANTS: T

Tweety's train — Tt Tt Tt

table	dishes	tiger	top
bone	Taz	ten	teeth
toaster	toothbrush	pumpkin	turtle

Directions: Have your child look at the picture in the first row and say Tweety's train while listening for the beginning t sound. Ask your child to name the pictures, then circle those that begin with the same t sound as the first picture. Your child should trace and write Tt in the space provided. Skill: Identifying the beginning sound t.

37

REVIEW

Quentin Q	quack	ladder	question mark
Ralph R	puppet	rattle	roof
Sam S	soap	carrot	scissors
Tweety T	top	turkey	pencil

38

Directions: Have your child say the letter and name the character at the beginning of each row. Then ask your child to circle each picture in the row whose name begins with the sound made by that letter. Skill: Identifying the beginning sounds q, r, s and t.

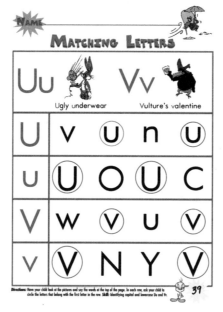

MATCHING LETTERS

Uu — Ugly underwear
Vv — Vulture's valentine

U	V	u	n	u
u	U	O	U	C
V	W	V	u	V
v	V	N	Y	V

Directions: Have your child look at the pictures and say the words at the top of the page. In each row, ask your child to circle the letters that belong with the first letter in the row. Skill: Identifying capital and lowercase Uu and Vv.

39

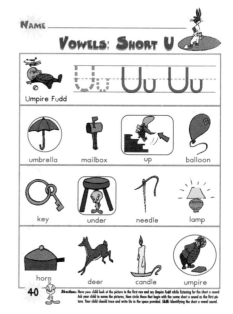

VOWELS: SHORT U

Umpire Fudd — Uu Uu Uu

umbrella	mailbox	up	balloon
key	under	needle	lamp
horn	deer	candle	umpire

40

Directions: Have your child look at the picture in the first row and say Umpire Fudd while listening for the short u sound. Ask your child to name the pictures, then circle those that begin with the same short u sound as the first picture. Your child should trace and write Uu in the space provided. Skill: Identifying the short u vowel sound.

ANSWER KEY

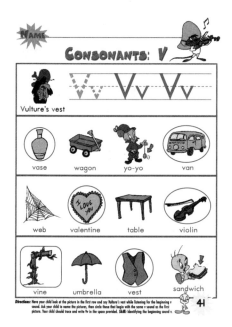

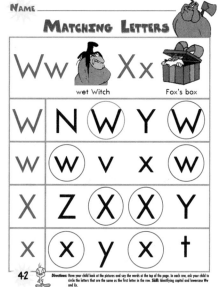

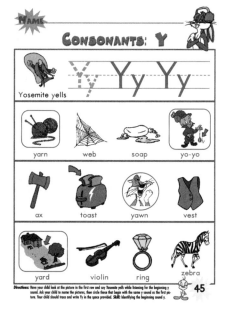

ANSWER KEY

REVIEW

Vulture	vest	web	van
Wile E.	well	wagon	zoo
Fox	yawn	ax	ox
Yosemite Sam	yo-yo	yarn	vase
Taz	zebra	valentine	zipper

Directions: Have your child say the letter and name the character at the beginning of each row. Then ask your child to circle each picture in the row whose name has the sound made by that letter. **Skill:** Identifying the beginning sounds v, w, x, y and z; the final sound x.

47

VOWELS: LONG A

ā   ape

rake	bag	safe
cage	skate	cat
van	paper	gate

48 **Directions:** Have your child look at the picture at the top of the page and say the word ape while listening for the long a vowel sound. Ask your child to name the other pictures, then circle those with the same long a sound. **Skill:** Identifying the long a vowel sound.

VOWELS: LONG A

ā   cake

snake	bed	tape
plate	six	plane
cage	whale	rake

Directions: Have your child look at the picture at the top of the page and say the word cake while listening for the long a vowel sound. Ask your child to name the other pictures, then circle those with the same long a sound. **Skill:** Identifying the long a vowel sound.

49

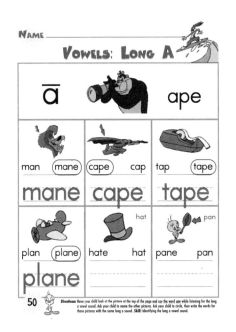

VOWELS: LONG A

ā   ape

man (mane)	(cape) cap	tap (tape)
mane	cape	tape
plan (plane)	hate hat / hat	pane pan / pan
plane		

50 **Directions:** Have your child look at the picture at the top of the page and say the word ape while listening for the long a vowel sound. Ask your child to name the other pictures. Ask your child to circle, then write the words for these pictures with the same long a sound. **Skill:** Identifying the long a vowel sound.

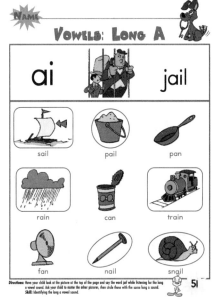

VOWELS: LONG A

ai   jail

sail	pail	pan
rain	can	train
fan	nail	snail

Directions: Have your child look at the picture at the top of the page and say the word jail while listening for the long a vowel sound. Ask your child to name the other pictures, then circle those with the same long a sound. **Skill:** Identifying the long a vowel sound.

51

VOWELS: LONG A

ai   nail

mail	rug	sail
mail	r g	sail
pail	tail	box
pail	tail	b x

52 **Directions:** Have your child look at the picture at the top of the page and say the word nail while listening for the long a vowel sound. Ask your child to name the other pictures, then write ai if the words have the same long a sound. **Skill:** Identifying the long a vowel sound.

Answer Key

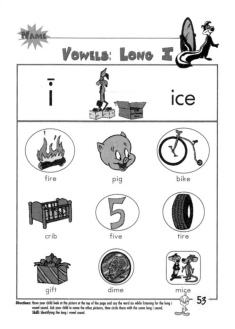

Vowels: Long I

ī — ice

- fire
- pig
- bike
- crib
- five
- tire
- gift
- dime
- mice

Directions: Have your child look at the picture at the top of the page and say the word *ice* while listening for the long i vowel sound. Ask your child to name the other pictures, then circle those with the same long i sound.
Skill: Identifying the long i vowel sound.

53

Vowels: Long I

ī — hive

- slide
- rollerblade
- bride
- wig
- pie
- tire
- nine
- spider
- kite

54

Directions: Have your child look at the picture at the top of the page and say the word *hive* while listening for the long i vowel sound. Ask your child to name the other pictures, then circle those with the same long i sound.
Skill: Identifying the long i vowel sound.

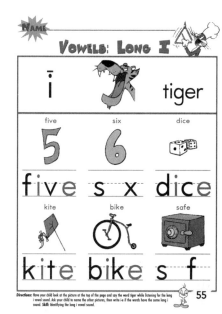

Vowels: Long I

ī — tiger

- five — 5
- six — 6
- dice
- five
- s x
- dice
- kite
- bike
- safe
- kite
- bike
- s f

Directions: Have your child look at the picture at the top of the page and say the word *tiger* while listening for the long i vowel sound. Ask your child to name the other pictures, then write i e if the words have the long i sound. Skill: Identifying the long i vowel sound.

55

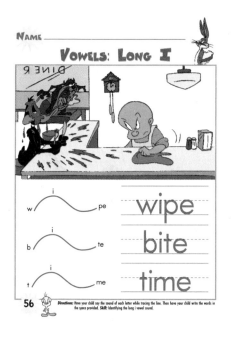

Vowels: Long I

- w — i — pe : wipe
- b — i — te : bite
- t — i — me : time

56

Directions: Have your child say the sound of each letter while tracing the line. Then have your child write the words in the space provided. Skill: Identifying the long i vowel sound.

Vowels: Long O

oa — soap

- boat
- soap
- toast
- fox
- coat
- road
- coach
- sock
- pan

Directions: Have your child look at the picture at the top of the page and say the word *soap* while listening for the long o vowel sound. Ask your child to name the other pictures, then circle those with the same long o sound.
Skill: Identifying the long o vowel sound.

57

Vowels: Long O

oa — toast

- croak
- vine
- coal
- soap
- roast
- snail
- spider
- road
- goal

58

Directions: Have your child look at the picture at the top of the page and say the word *toast* while listening for the long o vowel sound. Ask your child to name the other pictures, then circle those with the same long o sound.
Skill: Identifying the long o vowel sound.

Answer Key

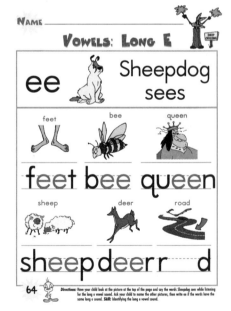

ANSWER KEY

PRACTICE PAGE

Directions: Use this space to practice skills learned in the previous pages.

PRACTICE PAGE

Directions: Use this space to practice skills learned in the previous pages.

79

PRACTICE PAGE

Directions: Use this space to practice skills learned in the previous pages.

NAME _____

PRACTICE PAGE

Directions: Use this space to practice skills learned in the previous pages.

Kindergarten

Thinking Skills

Opposites • Patterns • Comparisons

A McGraw·Hill/Warner Bros. Workbook

Table of Contents

Table of Contents (continued)

LEFT TO RIGHT

Directions: Have your child draw a line from left to right to connect the characters with the places they are going. **Skill:** Tracking objects from left to right.

LEFT TO RIGHT

Directions: Have your child draw a line from left to right to connect each animal with its favorite food.
Skill: Tracking objects from left to right.

TOP TO BOTTOM

TOP

Directions: Have your child draw a line from top to bottom to connect each balloon with the character that is holding it. **Skill:** Tracking objects from top to bottom.

BOTTOM

NAME

FOLLOWING DIRECTIONS

88

Directions: Have your child add the fishing line to the carrot, color Elmer's hat brown, then trace the dotted lines to make each soap bubble. **Skill:** Following directions.

SAME

	  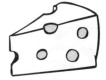

Directions: Have your child look at the first picture in each row, then circle the picture in the row that is the same. **Skill:** Identifying and matching objects that are the same.

DIFFERENT

90

Directions: Have your child look at each group of animals, then circle the animal that is different and finish coloring the picture. **Skill:** Identifying objects that are different.

NAME

LONG, SHORT

Directions: Have your child look at the pictures, then circle the short object in each row.
Skill: Identifying and comparing lengths of objects (long/short).

LONG, SHORT

Directions: Have your child look at the pictures, then circle the character with the long object in each row.
Skill: Identifying and comparing lengths of objects (long/short).

WIDE, NARROW

Directions: Have your child look at the pictures, then circle the wide object in each row. **Skill:** Identifying and comparing widths of objects (wide/narrow).

NAME

TALL, SHORT

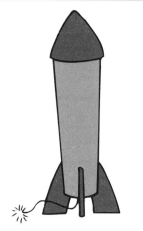

94

Directions: Have your child look at the pictures, then circle the tall object in each box. ***Skill:*** Identifying and comparing heights of objects (tall/short).

Heavy, Light

Directions: Have your child look at the pictures, then circle the heavier object in each box.
Skill: Identifying and comparing weights of objects (heavy/light).

95

THICK, THIN

Directions: Have your child look at the pictures, then circle the character with the thick object in each row. **Skill:** Identifying and comparing the thickness of objects (thick/thin).

PATTERNS

Directions: Have your child study the patterns in each row, then color in the shapes to continue each color pattern. **Skill:** Identifying and completing patterns.

PATTERNS

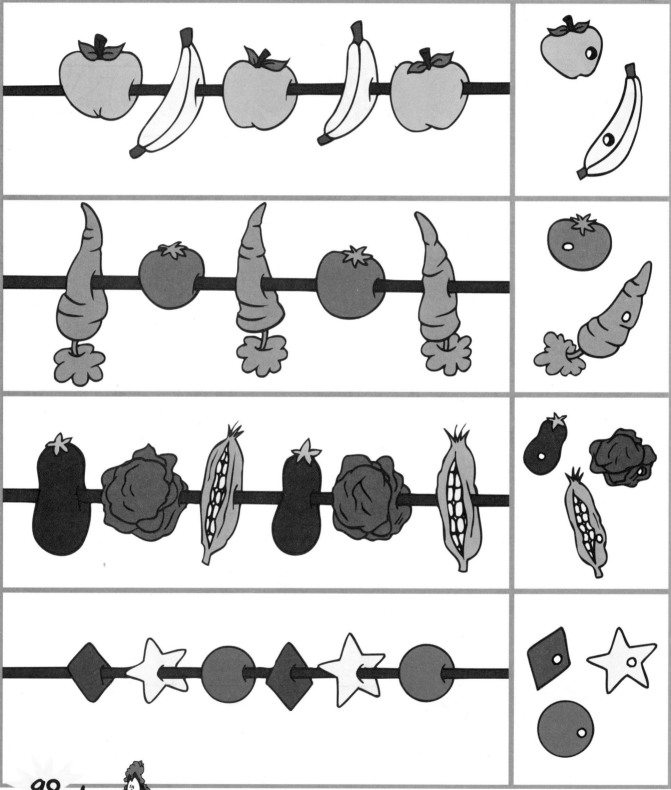

Directions: Have your child study the patterns in each row, then circle the object that comes next in each pattern. **Skill:** Identifying and completing patterns.

| X | O | X | O | X | | | | |

| O
O | X
X | O
O | X
X | O
O | | | | |

| O
O | X | O
O | X | O
O | | | | |

| X
X | O | X
X | O | X
X | | | | |

| X | O
O | X | O
O | X | | | | |

Directions: Have your child study the patterns in each row, then complete the patterns by filling in the spaces with the correct objects. **Skill:** Identifying and completing patterns.

PATTERNS

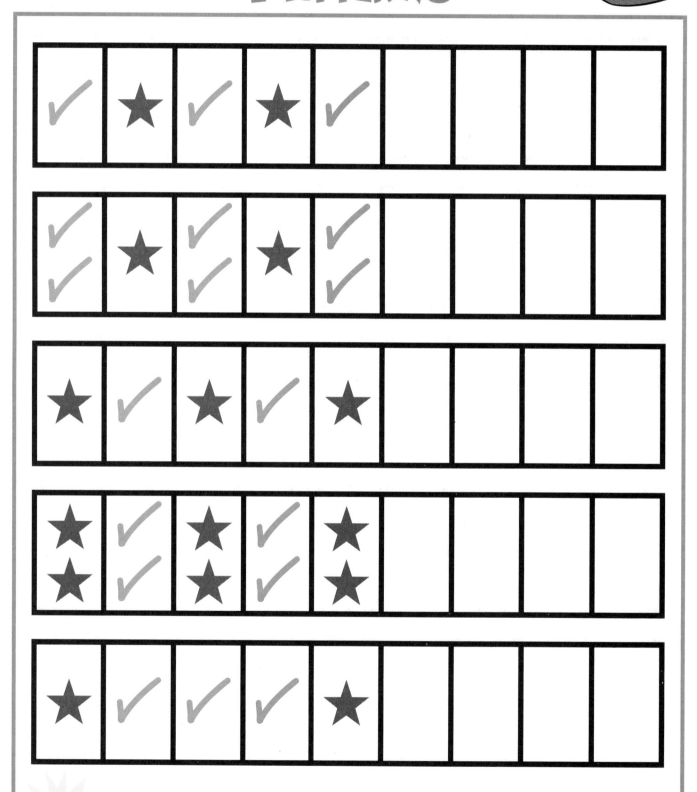

Directions: Have your child study the patterns in each row, then complete the patterns by filling in the spaces with the correct objects. **Skill:** Identifying and completing patterns.

PATTERNS

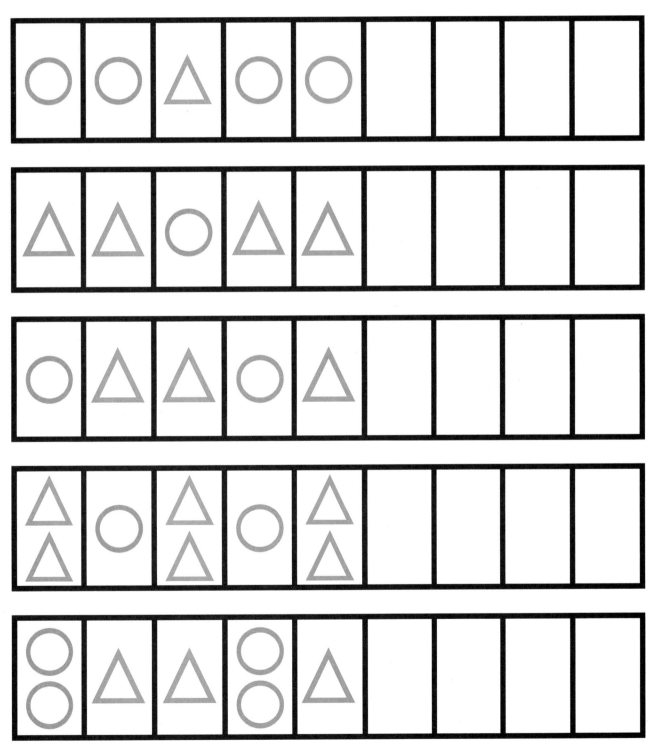

Directions: Have your child study the patterns in each row, then complete the patterns by filling in the spaces with the correct objects. **Skill:** Identifying and completing patterns.

101

NAME

PATTERNS

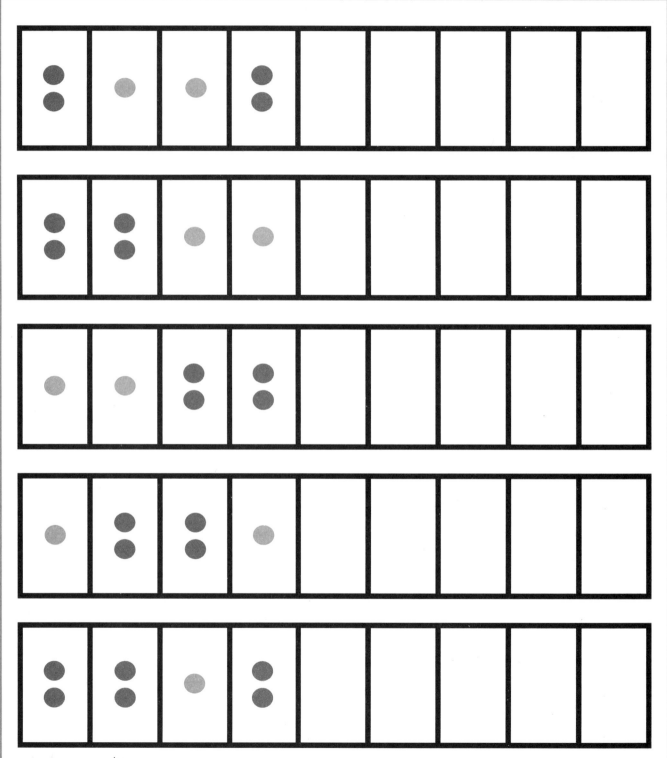

Directions: Have your child study the patterns in each row, then complete the patterns by filling in the spaces with the correct objects. **Skill:** Identifying and completing patterns.

PATTERNS

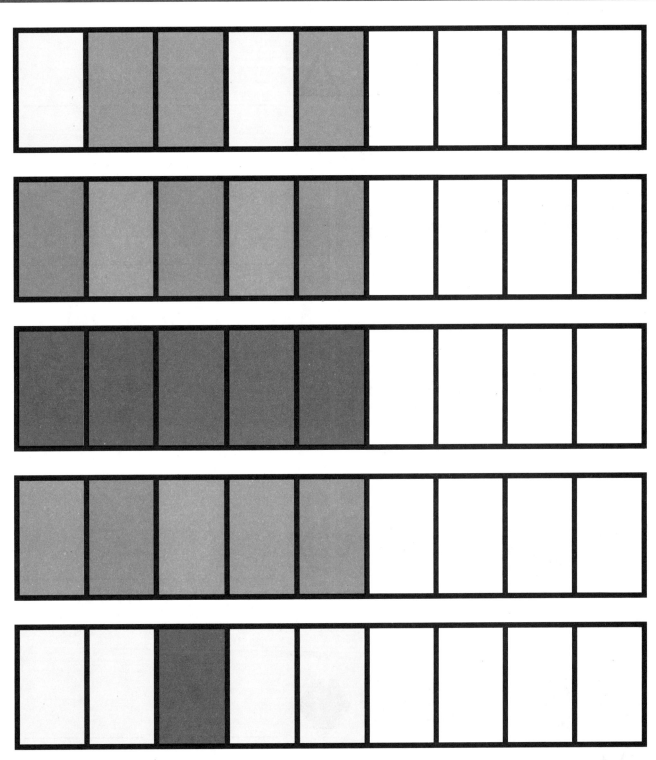

Directions: Have your child study the patterns in each row, then complete the patterns by filling in the spaces with the correct colors. **Skill:** Identifying and completing patterns.

PATTERNS

Directions: Have your child study the patterns in each row, then complete the patterns by filling in the spaces with the correct shapes. **Skill:** Identifying and completing patterns.

PATTERNS

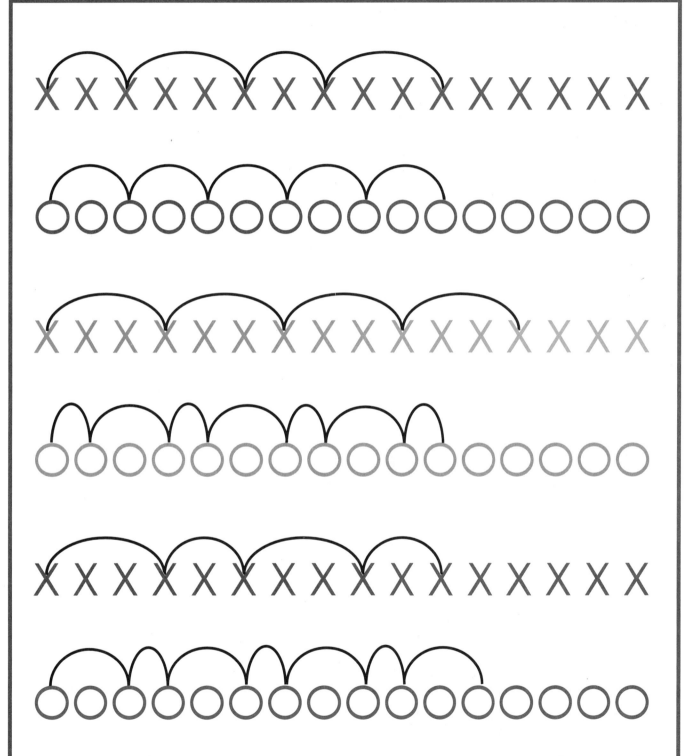

Directions: Have your child study the patterns in each row, then complete the patterns by continuing the lines. **Skill:** Identifying and completing patterns.

Patterns

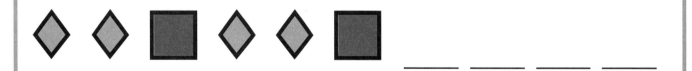

Directions: Have your child study the patterns in each row, then complete the patterns by filling in the spaces with the correct shapes. *Skill:* Identifying and completing patterns.

CLASSIFYING

Directions: Have your child look at the top half of the page and draw lines to show what belongs in Bugs Bunny's refrigerator. Have your child look at the bottom half of the page and draw lines to show what belongs in Petunia Pig's closet. *Skill:* Recognizing and grouping objects.

CLASSIFYING

Directions: Have your child help Sylvester Jr. get ready for his baseball game by circling five things he will need to take with him (baseball, bat, cap, mitt, and shoes). **Skill:** Sorting and classifying objects.

DOES IT BELONG?

Directions: Have your child look at the picture, then circle the things that are wrong. **Skill:** Recognizing objects that do not belong.

109

NAME _____

WHAT'S MISSING?

Directions: Have your child identify, then draw, what is missing in each picture. **Skill:** Identifying missing elements.

NAME _____

CLASSIFYING

Directions: Have your child draw a line from the candy to the jar where it belongs. **Skill:** Recognizing and grouping things that are alike.

CLASSIFYING

Directions: Have your child draw a line from the boxes at the top of the page to the box at the bottom to show which team each Looney Tunes character is on. **Skill:** Recognizing and grouping things that are alike.

CLASSIFYING

Directions: Have your child draw a line from each of Granny's trophies on the table to the shelf where it belongs. **Skill:** Recognizing and grouping things that are alike.

CLASSIFYING

Directions: Have your child help Porky put away his dishes by drawing a line to the shelf where each type of dish belongs. **Skill:** Recognizing and grouping things that are alike.

Matching

Directions: Have your child draw a line to connect each bone on the left to the same kind of bone on the right. **Skill:** Matching like objects.

MATCHING

Directions: At the top of the page, have your child draw a line to connect each sock on the left to the same sock on the right. At the bottom of the page, ask your child to draw a line to connect each toy on the left with the same toy on the right. **Skill:** Matching like objects.

Matching

Directions: At the top of the page, have your child draw a line from each mouse on the left to the same mouse on the right. At the bottom of the page, ask your child to draw a line from each bird on the left to the same bird on the right. ***Skill:*** Matching like objects.

Matching

Directions: Have your child draw a line from each object on the left to the same object on the right. Ask your child to circle the picture that has more objects. **Skill:** Matching like objects; identifying more.

MORE, LESS

Directions: Have your child draw a line from each partially hidden object in the picture on the left to the same object on the right. Ask your child to circle the picture that has more objects.
Skill: Matching like objects; identifying more.

119

Matching

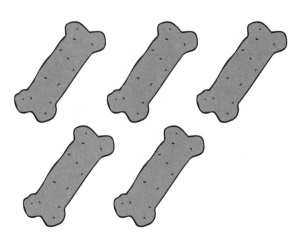

Directions: Have your child count the animals on the left, then circle the same number of objects on the right. **Skill:** Counting and matching objects.

Matching

Directions: At the top of the page, have your child draw lines connecting the puppies in the picture on the left with the puppies on the right. At the bottom of the page, ask your child to draw lines connecting the baby birds in the picture on the left to the baby birds on the right. Then have your child place an X on each picture that has more puppies and baby birds. **Skill:** Matching like objects; identifying more.

121

MORE

Directions: Have your child look at the pictures in each row, then circle the following: the bookcase with more books, the character that has more cannonballs, the tree that has more fruit.
Skill: Counting objects; identifying more.

LESS

Directions: Have your child look at the pictures in each row, then circle the following: the picture that has fewer pieces of pie, the picture that has fewer pieces of cheese, the picture that has fewer cats. **Skill:** Counting objects, identifying fewer (less).

123

BEGINNING SOUNDS

124

Directions: Have your child say each picture name, then draw a line between the objects if both picture names begin with the same sound. **Skill:** Identifying beginning consonant sounds.

BEGINNING SOUNDS

Directions: Have your child say the name of the first picture in each row and listen for the beginning
   sound. Then ask your child to circle the other pictures in the row whose names begin with the
   same sound. **Skill:** Identifying beginning consonant sounds.

RHYMING WORDS 2

Directions: Have your child name the pictures in each row, then circle the pictures whose names rhyme.
Skill: Identifying words that rhyme.

RHYMING WORDS

Directions: Have your child look at each scene, then circle the objects whose names rhyme.
    Skill: Identifying words that rhyme.

127

TOP, MIDDLE, BOTTOM

Directions: In each row, have your child circle the top character, put an X on the middle character and draw a box around the bottom character. ***Skill:*** Identifying the positions top, middle and bottom.

NAME

INSIDE, OUTSIDE

Directions: Have your child look at the cats at the top of the page and explain that one cat is inside the basket and the other cat is outside the basket. Ask your child to look at the cats on the rest of the page and put an X on the cats inside the baskets and circle the cats outside the baskets. ***Skill:*** Identifying the positions inside and outside.

LEFT TO RIGHT

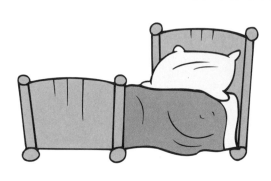 

Directions: In the top two boxes, have your child draw a path from left to right. Ask your child to make an X where he/she started. In the bottom two boxes, have your child draw a path from right to left. Ask your child to make an X to show where he/she started. **Skill:** Tracking items from left to right.

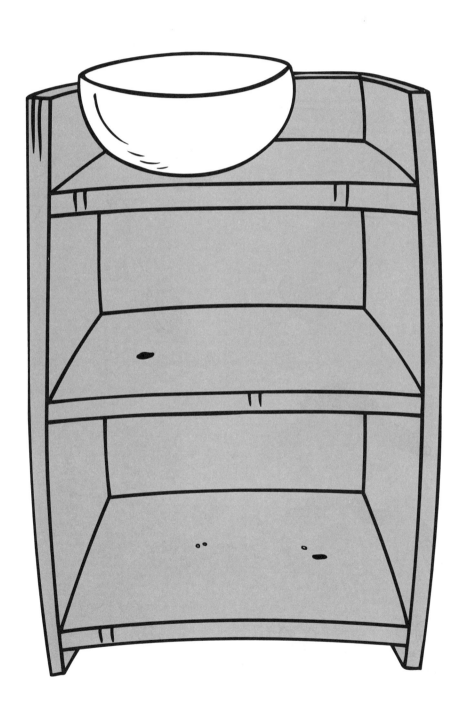

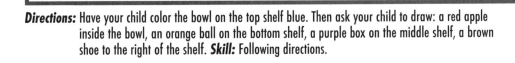 **Directions:** Have your child color the bowl on the top shelf blue. Then ask your child to draw: a red apple inside the bowl, an orange ball on the bottom shelf, a purple box on the middle shelf, a brown shoe to the right of the shelf. **Skill:** Following directions.

Same

Directions: Have your child circle the objects in each group that are the same. **Skill:** Identifying and matching objects that are the same.

SAME COLOR

Directions: Have your child look at the fruit on the left side of the page, then color the fruit on the right to match. **Skill:** Matching objects to the same color.

133

SAME SIZE

Directions: Have your child draw lines to match the objects that are the same size. **Skill:** Identifying and matching objects that are the same size.

 NAME

SAME SHAPE

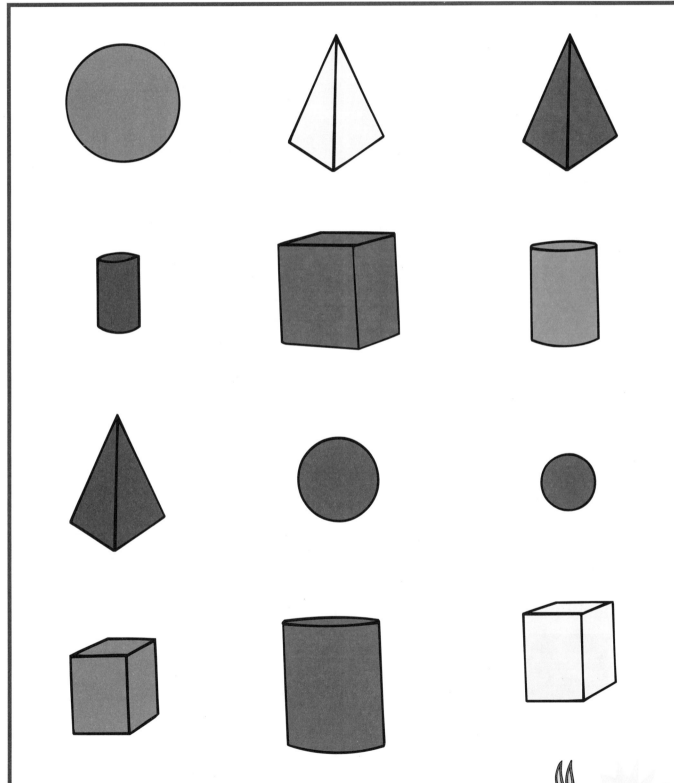

Directions: Have your child draw lines to match the objects that are the same shape. **Skill:** Identifying and matching objects that are the same shape.

DIFFERENT SHAPE

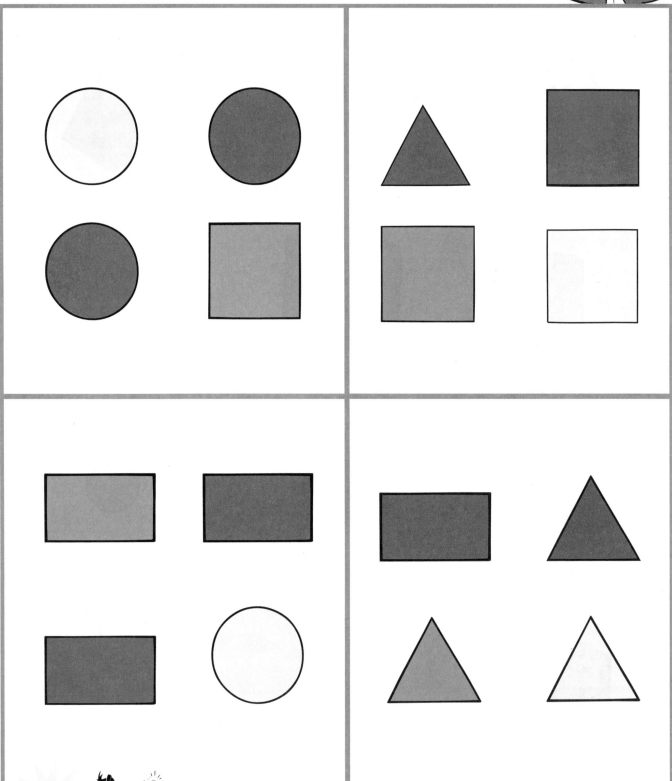

Directions: Have your child look at the shapes in each box, then circle the shape that is different.
Skill: Identifying objects that are different.

FOLLOWING DIRECTIONS

Directions: Have your child look at the picture, then: color the pillows that are the same shape orange, color the pillow that is a different shape green, circle the lamp that is a different size, put an X on the chair that is different, and circle the rug that is different. **Skill:** Following directions.

PATTERNS

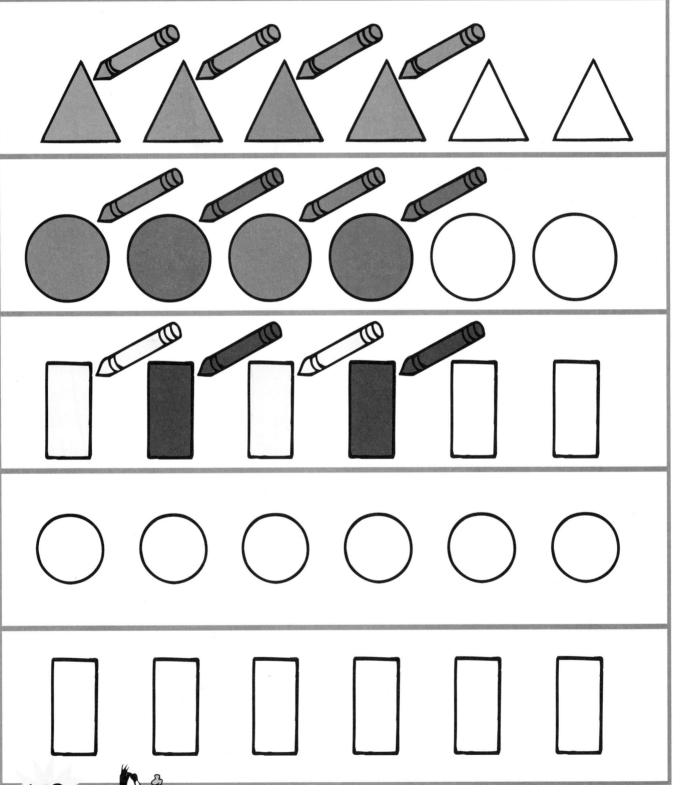

Directions: Have your child study the patterns in each row, then complete the patterns by filling in the objects with the correct color. Then ask your child to create original patterns in the bottom two rows. **Skill:** Identifying and completing patterns; creating original patterns.

PATTERNS

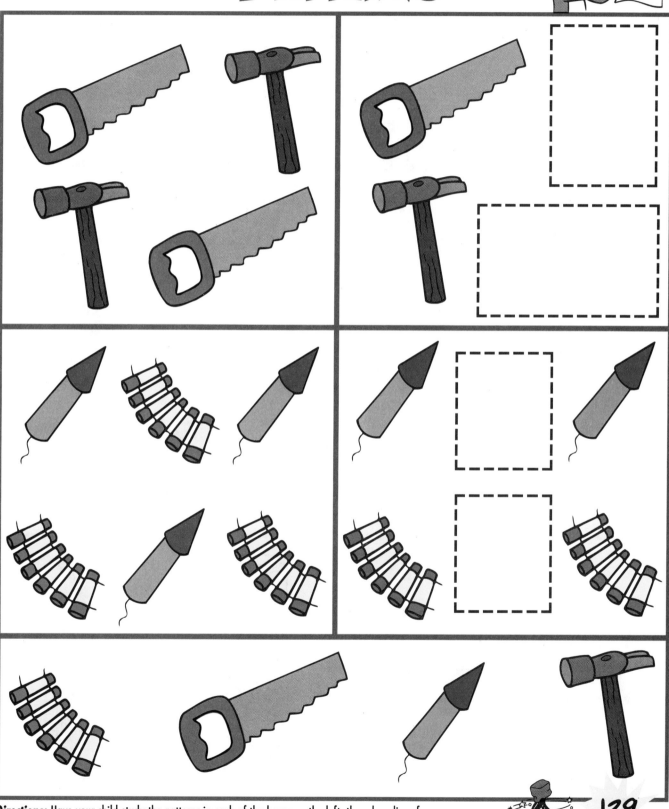

Directions: Have your child study the patterns in each of the boxes on the left, then draw lines from the objects at the bottom of the page to the correct boxes on the right. *Skill:* Identifying and completing patterns.

SAME NUMBER

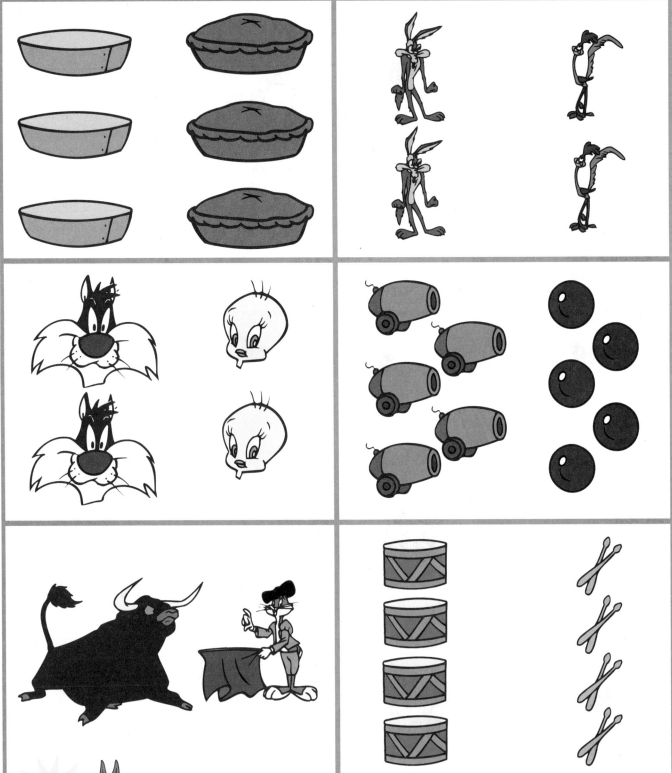

Directions: In each box, have your child draw lines from the objects on the left to the same number of objects on the right. **Skill:** Identifying and matching the same number of objects.

MORE

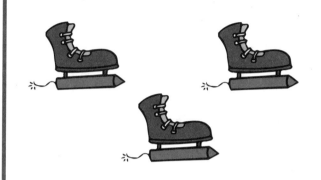

Directions: In each box, have your child draw lines from the objects on the top to the same number of objects below. Ask your child to circle the group within each box that has more objects.
Skill: Counting and matching objects; identifying more.

LESS

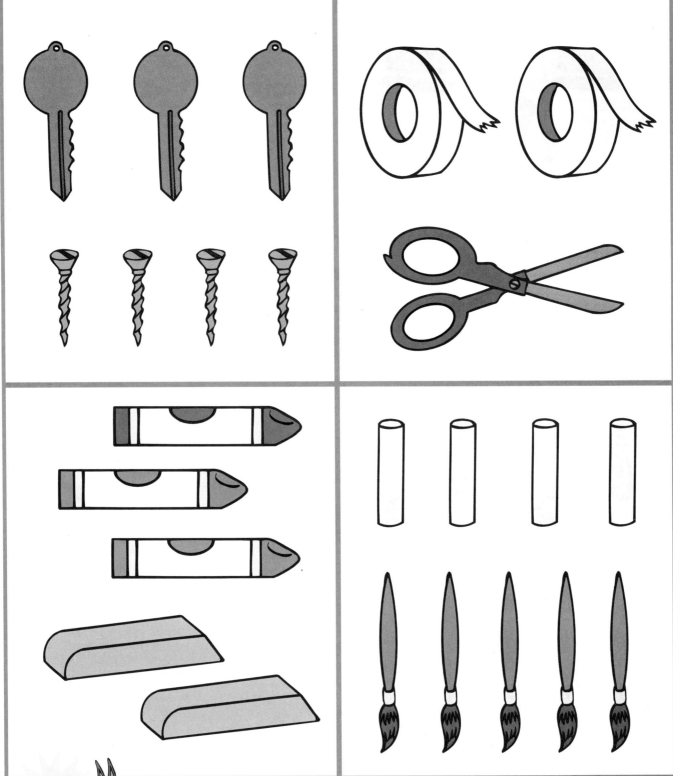

Directions: In each box, have your child draw lines from the objects on the top to the same number of objects below. Ask your child to circle the group that has fewer objects. **Skill:** Counting and matching objects; identifying fewer (less).

PATTERNS

Directions: Have your child color the first car in the first row red and the second car in the first row yellow. Ask your child to finish coloring the cars to complete the pattern. **Skill:** Identifying and completing patterns.

143

NAME _____

LONGER, SHORTER

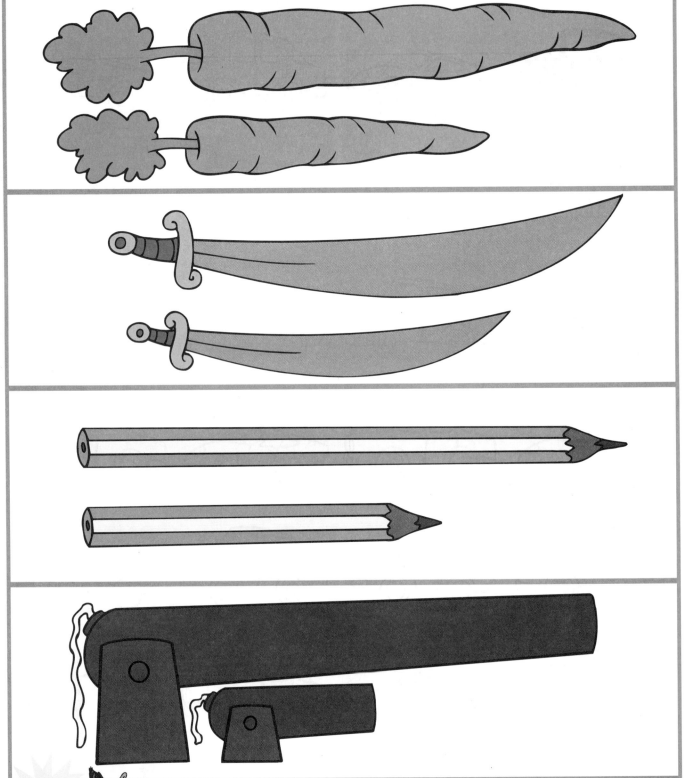

144

Directions: Have your child circle the longer object and put an X next to the shorter object.
Skill: Identifying and comparing lengths (longer/shorter).

TALLER, SHORTER

Directions: Have your child put an X on the taller tree and circle the shorter tree. **Skill:** Identifying and comparing heights (taller/shorter).

LONGEST, SHORTEST

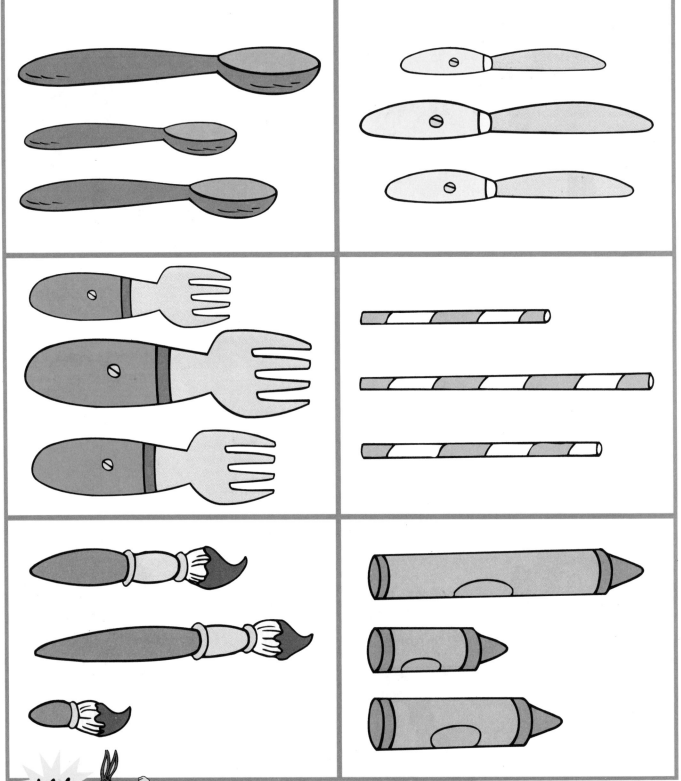

Directions: Have your child circle the shortest object and put an X on the longest object.
Skill: Identifying and comparing lengths (longest/shortest).

Answer Key

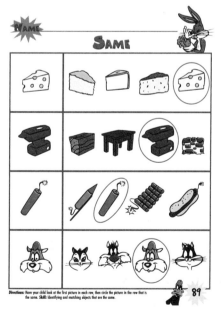

ANSWER KEY

Long, Short

Directions: Have your child look at the pictures, then circle the short object in each row.
Skill: Identifying and comparing lengths of objects (long/short).

Long, Short

Directions: Have your child look at the pictures, then circle the character with the long object in each row.
Skill: Identifying and comparing lengths of objects (long/short).

Wide, Narrow

Directions: Have your child look at the pictures, then circle the wide object in each row. **Skill:** Identifying and comparing widths of objects (wide/narrow).

Tall, Short

Directions: Have your child look at the pictures, then circle the tall object in each box. **Skill:** Identifying and comparing heights of objects (tall/short).

Heavy, Light

Directions: Have your child look at the pictures, then circle the heavier object in each box. **Skill:** Identifying and comparing weights of objects (heavy/light).

Thick, Thin

Directions: Have your child look at the pictures, then circle the character with the thick object in each row. **Skill:** Identifying and comparing the thickness of objects (thick/thin).

Answer Key

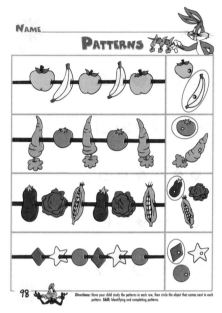

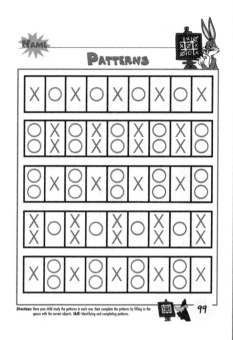

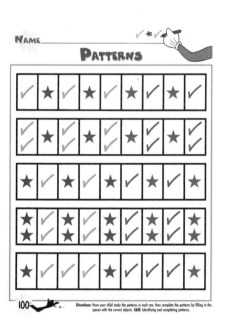

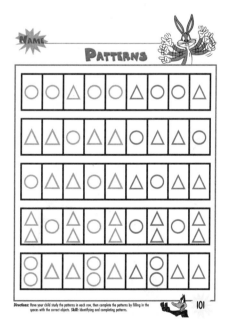

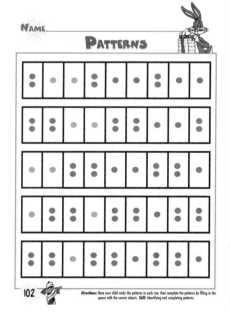

ANSWER KEY

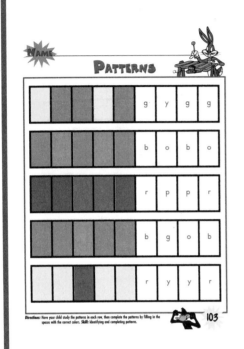

Directions: Have your child study the patterns in each row, then complete the patterns by filling in the spaces with the correct colors. Skill: Identifying and completing patterns.

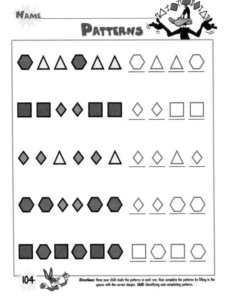

Directions: Have your child study the patterns in each row, then complete the patterns by filling in the spaces with the correct shapes. Skill: Identifying and completing patterns.

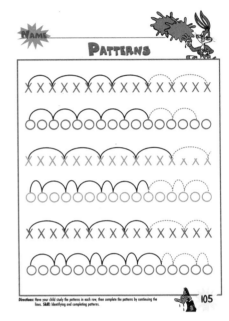

Directions: Have your child study the patterns in each row, then complete the patterns by continuing the lines. Skill: Identifying and completing patterns.

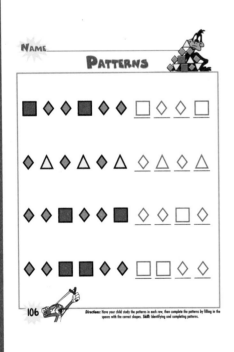

Directions: Have your child study the patterns in each row, then complete the patterns by filling in the spaces with the correct shapes. Skill: Identifying and completing patterns.

Directions: Have your child look at the top half of the page and draw lines to show what belongs in Bugs Bunny's refrigerator. Have your child look at the bottom half of the page and draw lines to show what belongs in Petunia Pig's closet. Skill: Recognizing and grouping objects.

Directions: Have your child help Sylvester Jr. get ready for his baseball game by circling five things he will need to take with him (baseball, bat, cap, mitt, and shoes). Skill: Sorting and classifying objects.

ANSWER KEY

DOES IT BELONG?

Directions: Have your child look at the picture, then circle the things that are wrong. *Skill:* Recognizing objects that do not belong.

109

WHAT'S MISSING?

Directions: Have your child identify, then draw, what is missing in each picture. *Skill:* Identifying missing elements.

110

CLASSIFYING

Directions: Have your child draw a line from the candy to the jar where it belongs. *Skill:* Recognizing and grouping things that are alike.

111

CLASSIFYING

Directions: Have your child draw a line from the boxes at the top of the page to the box at the bottom to show which team each Looney Tunes character is on. *Skill:* Recognizing and grouping things that are alike.

112

CLASSIFYING

Directions: Have your child draw a line from each of Granny's trophies on the table to the shelf where it belongs. *Skill:* Recognizing and grouping things that are alike.

113

CLASSIFYING

Directions: Have your child help Porky put away his dishes by drawing a line to the shelf where each type of dish belongs. *Skill:* Recognizing and grouping things that are alike.

114

151

ANSWER KEY

Directions: Have your child draw a line to connect each bone on the left to the same kind of bone on the right. **Skill:** Matching like objects.

115

116

Directions: At the top of the page, have your child draw a line to connect each sock on the left to the same sock on the right. At the bottom of the page, ask your child to draw a line to connect each toy on the left with the same toy on the right. **Skill:** Matching like objects.

Directions: At the top of the page, have your child draw a line from each mouse on the left to the same mouse on the right. At the bottom of the page, ask your child to draw a line from each bird on the left to the same bird on the right. **Skill:** Matching like objects.

117

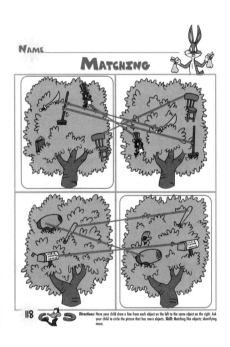

118

Directions: Have your child draw a line from each object on the left to the same object on the right. Ask your child to circle the picture that has more objects. **Skill:** Matching like objects; identifying more.

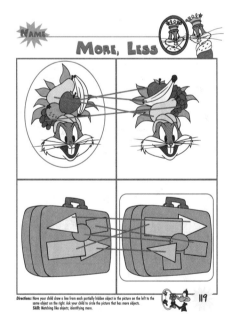

Directions: Have your child draw a line from each partially hidden object in the picture on the left to the same object on the right. Ask your child to circle the picture that has more objects. **Skill:** Matching like objects; identifying more.

119

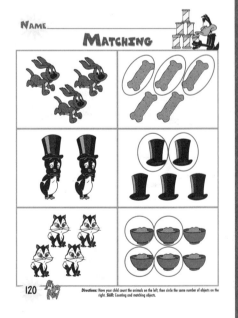

120

Directions: Have your child count the animals on the left, then circle the same number of objects on the right. **Skill:** Counting and matching objects.

ANSWER KEY

NAME

MATCHING

Directions: At the top of the page, have your child draw lines connecting the puppies in the picture on the left with the puppies on the right. At the bottom of the page, ask your child to draw lines connecting the baby birds in the picture on the left to the baby birds on the right. Then have your child place an X on each picture that has more puppies and baby birds. **Skill:** Matching like objects; identifying more.

121

NAME

MORE

122

Directions: Have your child look at the pictures in each row, then circle the following: the bookcase with more books, the character that has more cannonballs, the tree that has more fruit. **Skill:** Counting objects; identifying more.

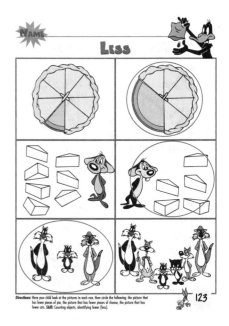

NAME

LESS

Directions: Have your child look at the pictures in each row, then circle the following: the picture that has fewer pieces of pie, the picture that has fewer pieces of cheese, the picture that has fewer cats. **Skill:** Counting objects; identifying fewer (less).

123

NAME

BEGINNING SOUNDS

cookie
wagon
crayon
lamp
ghost
bird
goat
bicycle
sun
jar
skunk
jet

124 **Directions:** Have your child say each picture name, then draw a line between the objects if both picture names begin with the same sound. **Skill:** Identifying beginning consonant sounds.

NAME

BEGINNING SOUNDS

turkey
tape
saw
turtle
tent
frog
fox
foot
heart
fish
Road Runner
ring
cat
rope
rug
house
horse
hose
hat
bird

Directions: Have your child say the name of the first picture in each row and listen for the beginning sound. Then ask your child to circle the other pictures in the row whose names begin with the same sound. **Skill:** Identifying beginning consonant sounds.

125

NAME

RHYMING WORDS

cat
hat
box
bat
block
sun
sock
clock
star
car
jar
bed
sail
nail
buzzard
pail

126 **Directions:** Have your child name the pictures in each row, then circle the pictures whose names rhyme. **Skill:** Identifying words that rhyme.

153

ANSWER KEY

RHYMING WORDS

pole
hole
horn
star
hot dog
frog
log
jar

Directions: Have your child look at each scene, then circle the objects whose names rhyme. **Skill:** Identifying words that rhyme.

127

TOP, MIDDLE, BOTTOM

Directions: In each row, have your child circle the top character, put an X on the middle character and draw a box around the bottom character. **Skill:** Identifying the positions top, middle and bottom.

128

INSIDE, OUTSIDE

Directions: Have your child look at the cats at the top of the page and explain that one cat is inside the basket and the other cat is outside the basket. Ask your child to look at the cats on the rest of the page and put an X on the cats inside the baskets and circle the cats outside the baskets. **Skill:** Identifying the positions inside and outside.

129

LEFT TO RIGHT

Directions: In the top two boxes, have your child draw a path from left to right. Ask your child to make an X where he/she started. In the bottom two boxes, have your child draw a path from right to left. Ask your child to make an X to show where he/she started. **Skill:** Tracking items from left to right.

130

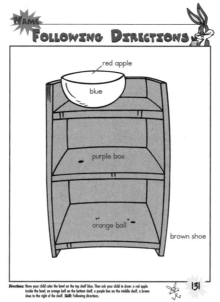

FOLLOWING DIRECTIONS

red apple
blue
purple box
orange ball
brown shoe

Directions: Have your child color the bowl on the top shelf blue. Then ask your child to draw: a red apple inside the bowl, an orange ball on the bottom shelf, a purple box on the middle shelf, a brown shoe to the right of the shelf. **Skill:** Following directions.

131

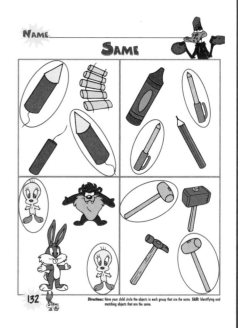

SAME

Directions: Have your child circle the objects in each group that are the same. **Skill:** Identifying and matching objects that are the same.

132

154

ANSWER KEY

NAME

SAME COLOR

Directions: Have your child look at the fruit on the left side of the page, then color the fruit on the right to match. **Skill:** Matching objects to the same color. **133**

SAME SIZE

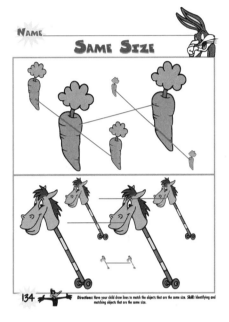

134 **Directions:** Have your child draw lines to match the objects that are the same size. **Skill:** Identifying and matching objects that are the same size.

SAME SHAPE

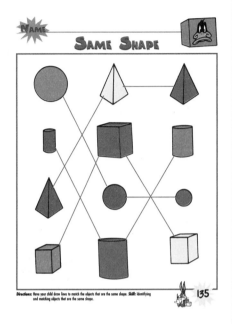

Directions: Have your child draw lines to match the objects that are the same shape. **Skill:** Identifying and matching objects that are the same shape. **135**

DIFFERENT SHAPE

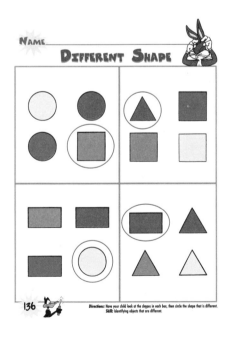

136 **Directions:** Have your child look at the shapes in each box, then circle the shape that is different. **Skill:** Identifying objects that are different.

FOLLOWING DIRECTIONS

Directions: Have your child look at the picture, then: color the pillows that are the same shape orange, color the pillow that is a different shape green, circle the lamp that is a different size, put an X on the chair that is different, and circle the rug that is different. **Skill:** Following directions. **137**

PATTERNS

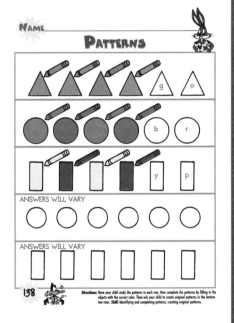

ANSWERS WILL VARY

ANSWERS WILL VARY

138 **Directions:** Have your child study the patterns in each row, then complete the patterns by filling in the objects with the correct color. Then ask your child to create original patterns in the bottom two rows. **Skill:** Identifying and completing patterns; creating original patterns.

155

Answer Key

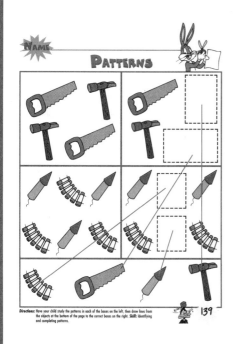

Patterns

139

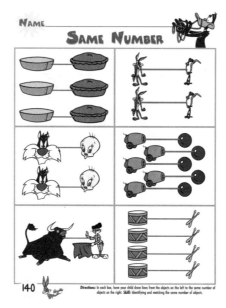

Same Number

140

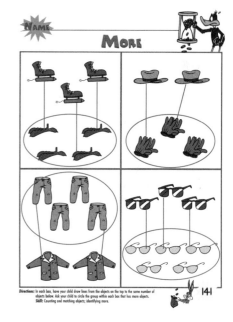

More

141

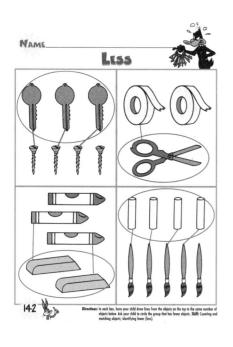

Less

142

Patterns

143

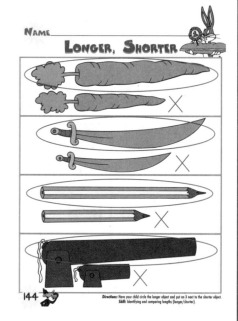

Longer, Shorter

144

156

ANSWER KEY

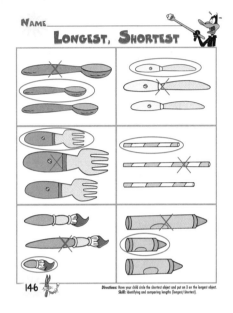

PRACTICE PAGE

Directions: Use this space to practice skills learned in the previous pages.

PRACTICE PAGE

Directions: Use this space to practice skills learned in the previous pages.

PRACTICE PAGE

 Directions: Use this space to practice skills learned in the previous pages.

NAME

PRACTICE PAGE

Directions: Use this space to practice skills learned in the previous pages.

The Nation's #1 Educational Publisher

The McGraw·Hill Companies

Kindergarten

**Phonics • Vocabulary
Comprehension • Writing**

A McGraw·Hill/Warner Bros. Workbook

Table of Contents

Table of Contents (continued)

TOP, BOTTOM

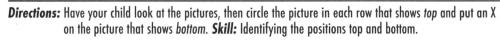

Directions: Have your child look at the pictures, then circle the picture in each row that shows *top* and put an X on the picture that shows *bottom*. ***Skill:*** Identifying the positions top and bottom.

165

LEFT, RIGHT

Directions: Have your child look at the picture, then color the ball on the *left* green, color the ball on the *right* red, then circle the characters on the *left*. **Skill:** Identifying the positions left and right.

MATCHING

s	s	e	s	w
i	l	i	i	y
p	p	d	b	p
b	b	c	b	d
G	D	G	Q	G
N	N	R	N	M
Y	J	Y	P	Y
J	J	P	J	I

Directions: Have your child look at the letter in the box at the beginning of each row, then circle the two letters in each row that are the same. *Skill:* Matching capital and lowercase letters.

NUMBERS 1 TO 10

1 2 3 4 5

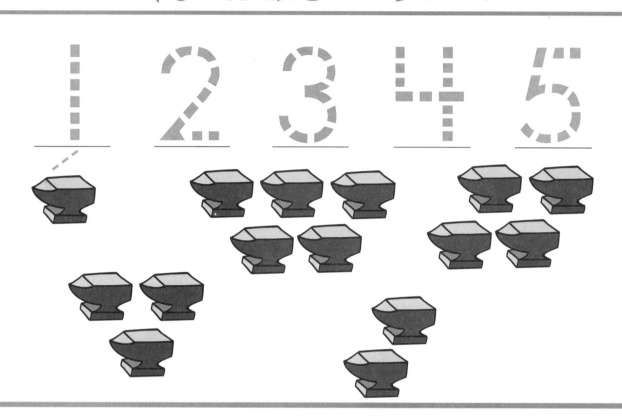

6 7 8 9 10

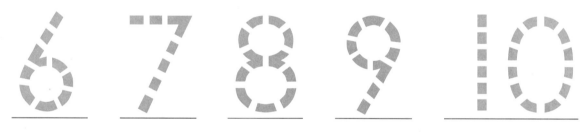

168

Directions: Have your child trace each number, then draw a line from the number to the set of anvils or horseshoes it represents. **Skill:** Writing the numbers 1 to 10; recognizing groups of 1 to 10.

BEGINNING SOUND K

Directions: Have your child trace Kk at the beginning of each row. Ask your child to name the pictures, then circle those with the beginning sound k. **Skill:** Identifying the beginning sound k; writing Kk.

COMPREHENSION

The the

the

The

Directions: Have your child identify the word at the top of the page, then trace and write the words and sentences. Point out the use of capital letters and periods in the sentences. **Skill:** Understanding and using vocabulary; recognizing sentence structure.

Directions: Have your child trace Mm at the beginning of each row. Ask your child to name the pictures, then circle those with the beginning sound m. **Skill:** Identifying the beginning sound m; writing Mm.

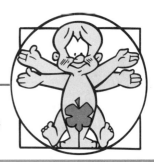

COMPREHENSION

The the man

the

The man

.

.

Directions: Have your child identify the words at the top of the page, then trace and write the words and sentences. Point out the use of capital letters and periods in the sentences. **Skill:** Understanding and using vocabulary; recognizing sentence structure.

BEGINNING SOUND B

B b		
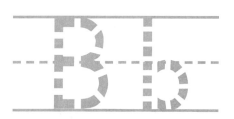		
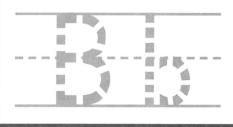		

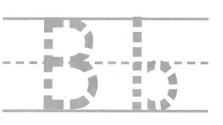	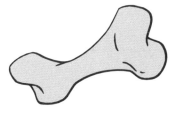	

Directions: Have your child trace Bb at the beginning of each row. Ask your child to name the pictures, then circle those with the beginning sound b. *Skill:* Identifying the beginning sound b; writing Bb.

173

COMPREHENSION

Boys boys

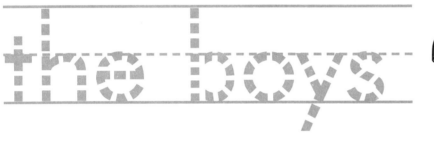

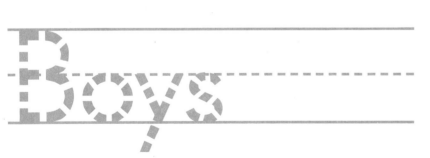

Directions: Have your child identify the word at the top of the page, then trace and write the words and sentences. Point out the use of capital letters and periods in the sentences. **Skill:** Understanding and using vocabulary; recognizing sentence structure.

Sequence

Directions: Have your child identify the scenes in each box, then ask your child to number the pictures in the order in which they take place. **Skill:** Identifying a sequence of events.

175

VOWELS: SHORT A

A a   c a t

Directions: Have your child trace Aa at the beginning of each row. Ask your child to say the word *cat* while listening for the short a sound. Have your child name the pictures, then circle those that have the same short a sound as the picture at the top of the page. ***Skill:*** Identifying the short a vowel sound; writing Aa.

COMPREHENSION

The the man

Boys boys

the boys

Boys

The man

Directions: Have your child identify the words at the top of the page, then trace and write the words and sentences. Point out the use of capital letters and periods in the sentences. **Skill:** Understanding and using vocabulary; recognizing sentence structure.

177

CLASSIFYING

Directions: Have your child identify the pictures, then circle those in each box that belong in the same category: the cat family, things to sit on, things to play with and things to ride. **Skill:** Identifying and classifying objects.

First, Middle, Last

Directions: Have your child identify the pictures, then circle the *last* character in the first row; the *middle* character in the second row, the *first* train in the third row and the *middle* character in the fourth row.

Skill: Identifying the positions first, middle and last.

179

BEGINNING SOUND J

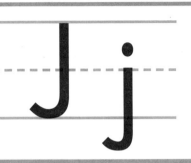

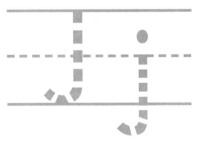

Directions: Have your child trace Jj at the beginning of each row. Ask your child to name the pictures, then circle those with the beginning sound j. **Skill:** Identifying the beginning sound j; writing Jj.

COMPREHENSION

Jump jump

The boys jump.

Jump boys!

181

Directions: Have your child identify the word at the top of the page, then trace and write the words and sentences. Point out the use of capital letters, periods and exclamation points in the sentences.
Skill: Understanding and using vocabulary; recognizing sentence structure.

BEGINNING SOUND F

 **2** **5**

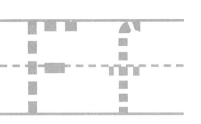  

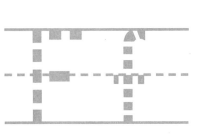  

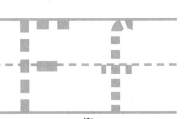  

Directions: Have your child trace Ff at the beginning of each row. Ask your child to name the pictures, then circle those with the beginning sound f. **Skill:** Identifying the beginning sound f; writing Ff.

COMPREHENSION

fish

Boys fish.

The boys fish.

Directions: Have your child identify the word at the top of the page, then trace and write the words and sentences. Point out the use of capital letters and periods in the sentences. **Skill:** Understanding and using vocabulary; recognizing sentence structure.

BEGINNING SOUND G

G g

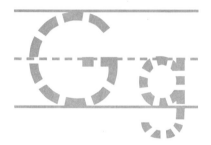  

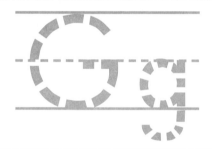  

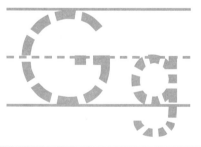  

Directions: Have your child trace Gg at the beginning of each row. Ask your child to name the pictures, then circle those with the beginning sound g. **Skill:** Identifying the beginning sound g; writing Gg.

Girls   girls

Girls jump.

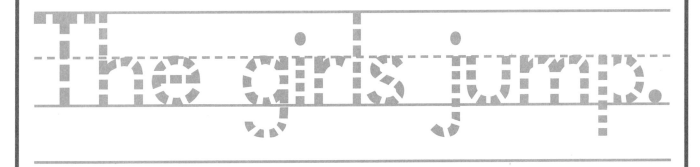

The girls jump.

185

Directions: Have your child identify the word at the top of the page, then trace and write the words and sentences. Point out the use of capital letters and periods in the sentences. **Skill:** Understanding and using vocabulary; recognizing sentence structure.

COMPREHENSION

and

girls and boys

_____

- - - - - - - - - - - - - - - - -

_____

_____

- - - - - - - - - - - - -

Girls _____ boys jump.

Directions: Have your child identify the word at the top of the page, then trace and write the words and sentences. Point out the use of the capital letter and period in the sentence. **Skill:** Understanding and using vocabulary; recognizing sentence structure.

Sequence

Directions: Ask your child to identify the pictures in each group, then number the pictures in the order in which they take place. **Skill:** Identifying a sequence of events.

VOWELS: SHORT E

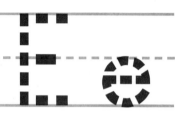 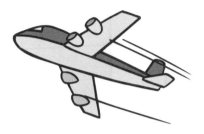 

jet

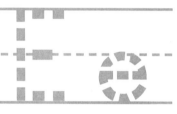   

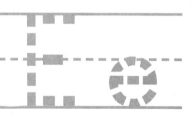  10

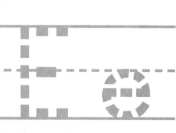   

Directions: Have your child trace Ee at the beginning of each row. Ask your child to say the word *jet* while listening for the short e sound. Have your child name the pictures, then circle those that have the same short e sound as the picture at the top of the page. **Skill:** Identifying the short e vowel sound; writing Ee.

COMPREHENSION

Girls __ boys fish.

and   the

Boys and __ jump.

fish   girls

__ girls!

Boys   Jump

The girls __.

fish   jump

Directions: Have your child look at the pictures in each box, then circle the word that completes the sentence and describes the picture. **Skill:** Understanding and using vocabulary; recognizing sentence structure.

189

CLASSIFYING

Directions: Have your child identify the pictures, then circle those in each box that belong in the same category: things a cowboy uses, the cat family, people who work in the city, and things that grow.
Skill: Identifying and classifying objects.

Sequence

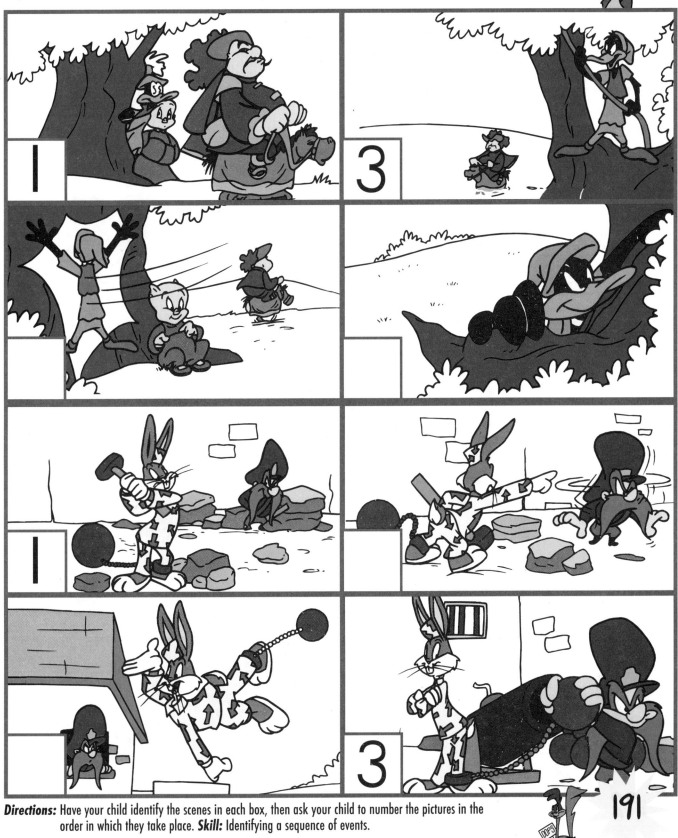

Directions: Have your child identify the scenes in each box, then ask your child to number the pictures in the order in which they take place. **Skill:** Identifying a sequence of events.

191

NAME _____

BEGINNING SOUND H

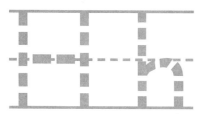  

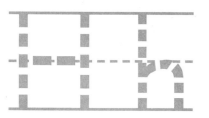  

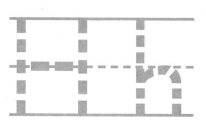  

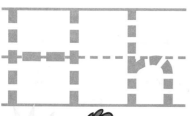  

Directions: Have your child trace Hh at the beginning of each row. Ask your child to name the pictures, then circle those with the beginning sound h. **Skill:** Identifying the beginning sound h; writing Hh.

NAME _____

BEGINNING SOUND R

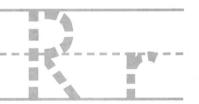  

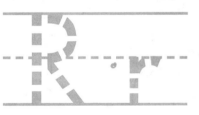  

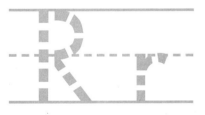  

Directions: Have your child trace Rr at the beginning of each row. Ask your child to name the pictures, then circle those with the beginning sound r. **Skill:** Identifying the beginning sound r; writing Rr.

193

COMPREHENSION

rides

rides

The man rides.

Directions: Have your child identify the word at the top of the page, then trace and write the words and sentences. Point out the use of capital letters and periods in the sentences. **Skill:** Understanding and using vocabulary; recognizing sentence structure.

BEGINNING SOUND N

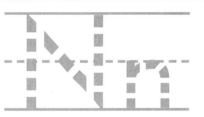		
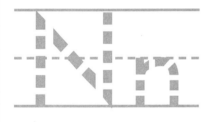		

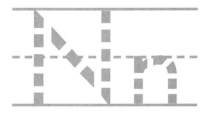		

Directions: Have your child trace Nn at the beginning of each row. Ask your child to name the pictures, then circle those with the beginning sound n. **Skill:** Identifying the beginning sound n; writing Nn.

COMPREHENSION

Now now

Jump now.

Now jump.

Directions: Have your child identify the word at the top of the page, then trace and write the words and sentences. Point out the use of capital letters and periods in the sentences. **Skill:** Understanding and using vocabulary; recognizing sentence structure.

NAME _____

BEGINNING SOUND S

S s

  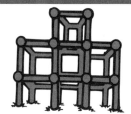

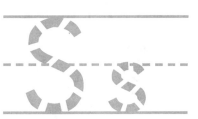  

197

Directions: Have your child trace Ss at the beginning of each row. Ask your child to name the pictures, then circle those with the beginning sound s. **Skill:** Identifying the beginning sound s; writing Ss.

COMPREHENSION

See see

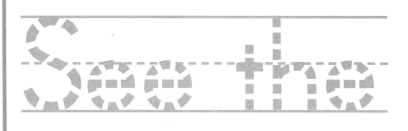 

BEGINNING SOUND P

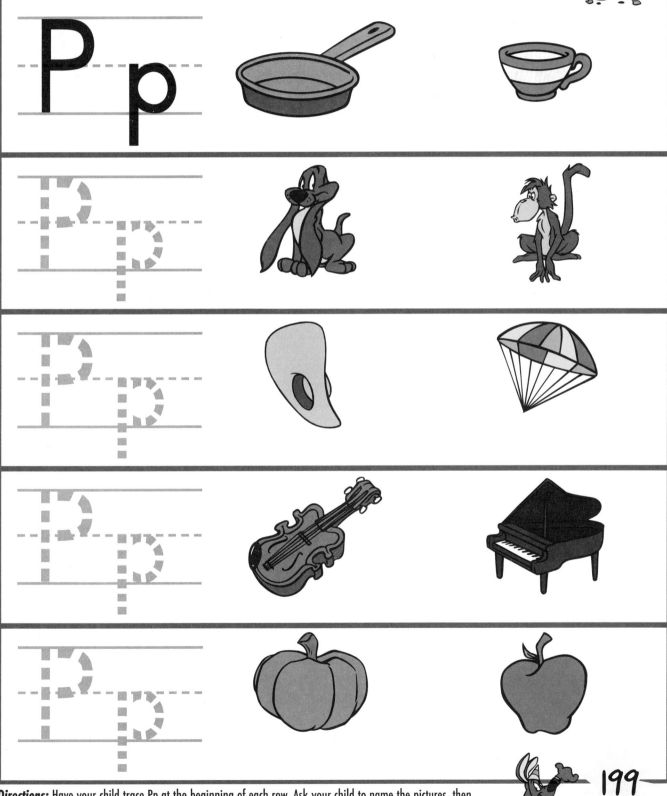

Directions: Have your child trace Pp at the beginning of each row. Ask your child to name the pictures, then circle those with the beginning sound p. **Skill:** Identifying the beginning sound p; writing Pp.

COMPREHENSION

park

the park

See the park!

Directions: Have your child identify the word at the top of the page, then trace and write the words and sentences. Point out the use of capital letters and exclamation points in the sentences.
Skill: Understanding and using vocabulary; recognizing sentence structure.

VOWELS: SHORT U

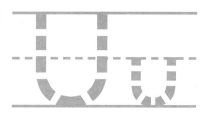   

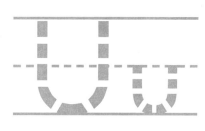   

201

Directions: Have your child trace Uu at the beginning of each row. Ask your child to say the word *cup* while listening for the short u sound. Have your child name the pictures, then circle those that have the same short u sound as the picture at the top of the page. **Skill:** Identifying the short u vowel sound; writing Uu.

COMPREHENSION

The man __.
rides   boys

Jump __!
park   now

See the __.
park   fish

Now the boys __.
jump   see

Directions: Have your child look at the pictures in each box, then circle the word that completes the sentence and describes the picture. **Skill:** Understanding and using vocabulary; recognizing sentence structure.

NAME  _____

Matching

Directions: Have your child name the pictures, then circle the picture that is related to the picture at the beginning of each row. **Skill:** Identifying and matching pairs of pictures.

BEGINNING SOUND C

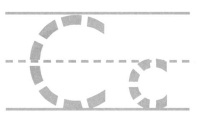  

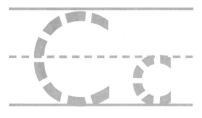  

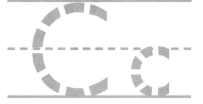  

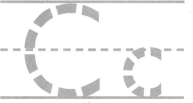  

Directions: Have your child trace Cc at the beginning of each row. Ask your child to name the pictures, then circle those with the beginning sound c. **Skill:** Identifying the beginning sound c; writing Cc.

Can can

Can Can

can can

_____ the man fish?

The man _____ fish.

205

Directions: Have your child identify the word at the top of the page. Ask your child to trace and write the words, then place them in the sentences at the bottom of the page. Point out the use of capital letters, the question mark and the period in the sentences. **Skill:** Understanding and using vocabulary; recognizing sentence structure.

BEGINNING SOUND Y

  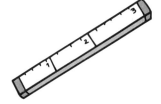

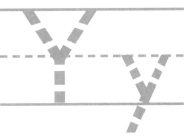  

Directions: Have your child trace Yy at the beginning of each row. Ask your child to name the pictures, then circle those with the beginning sound y. **Skill:** Identifying the beginning sound y; writing Yy.

You you

You can .

.

Can you ?

?

207

Directions: Have your child identify the word at the top of the page, then trace and write the words and sentences. Point out the use of capital letters, periods and question marks in the sentences.
Skill: Understanding and using vocabulary; recognizing sentence structure.

BEGINNING SOUND T

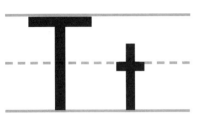  

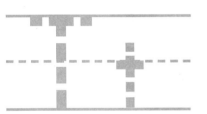  

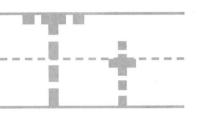  

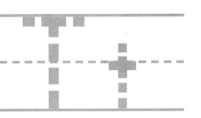  

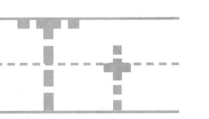  

Directions: Have your child trace Tt at the beginning of each row. Ask your child to name the pictures, then circle those with the beginning sound t. **Skill:** Identifying the beginning sound t; writing Tt.

COMPREHENSION

to

to   to   to

Jump to the .

Directions: Have your child identify the word at the top of the page, then trace and write the words and sentences. Point out the use of capital letters and periods in the sentences. **Skill:** Understanding and using vocabulary; recognizing sentence structure.

BEGINNING SOUND W

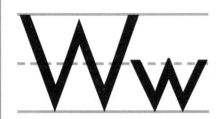  

Directions: Have your child trace Ww at the beginning of each row. Ask your child to name the pictures, then circle those with the beginning sound w. **Skill:** Identifying the beginning sound w; writing Ww.

BEGINNING SOUND Z

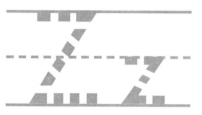  

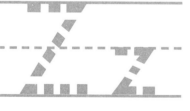

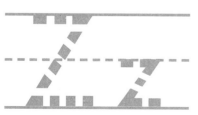  

211

Directions: Have your child trace Zz at the beginning of each row. Ask your child to name the pictures, then circle those with the beginning sound z. **Skill:** Identifying the beginning sound z; writing Zz.

COMPREHENSION

Directions: Have your child identify the pictures in each box and explain the sequence of events. Ask your child to draw a picture in the last box to show what happens next. **Skill:** Identifying a sequence of events; predicting an outcome.

VOWELS: SHORT I

Directions: Have your child trace Ii at the beginning of each row. Ask your child to say the word *dig* while listening for the short i sound. Have your child name the pictures, then circle those that have the same short i sound as the picture at the top of the page. **Skill:** Identifying the short i vowel sound; writing Ii.

COMPREHENSION

The man rides __ a park.

to   and

The man __ jump.

see   can

Can __ jump?

you   and

__ you see?

To   Can

Directions: Have your child identify the pictures in each box, then circle the word that completes the sentence and describes the picture. **Skill:** Understanding and using vocabulary; recognizing sentence structure.

Name _____

Beginning Sound L

215

Directions: Have your child trace Ll at the beginning of each row. Ask your child to name the pictures, then circle those with the beginning sound l. **Skill:** Identifying the beginning sound l; writing Ll.

COMPREHENSION

like

You like

You like to

Directions: Have your child identify the word at the top of the page, then trace and write the words and sentences. Point out the use of capital letters and periods in the sentences. **Skill:** Understanding and using vocabulary; recognizing sentence structure.

BEGINNING SOUND D

Dd

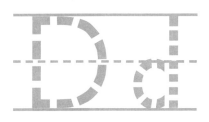  

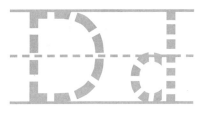 

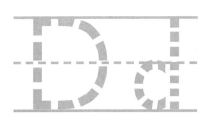  

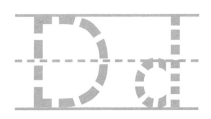 

Directions: Have your child trace Dd at the beginning of each row. Ask your child to name the pictures, then circle those with the beginning sound d. **Skill:** Identifying the beginning sound d; writing Dd.

217

NAME

down

down down

Jump down!

Directions: Have your child identify the word at the top of the page, then trace and write the words and sentences. Point out the use of capital letters and exclamation points in the sentences.
Skill: Understanding and using vocabulary; recognizing sentence structure.

NAME _____

BEGINNING SOUND V

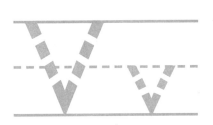  

219

Directions: Have your child trace Vv at the beginning of each row. Ask your child to name the pictures, then circle those with the beginning sound v. **Skill:** Identifying the beginning sound v; writing Vv.

BEGINNING SOUND Qu

Directions: Have your child trace Qu/qu at the beginning of each row. Ask your child to name the pictures, then circle those with the beginning sound qu. *Skill:* Identifying the beginning sound qu; writing Qu/qu.

FINAL SOUND X

 **8** **6**

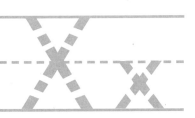  

221

Directions: Have your child trace Xx at the beginning of each row. Ask your child to name the pictures, then circle those with the final sound x. *Skill:* Identifying the final sound x; writing Xx.

COMPREHENSION

A man rides to ___a___ park.

_____ man rides to _____ park.

Directions: Have your child identify the word at the top of the page, then trace and write the sentences and words. Point out the use of capital letters and periods in the sentences. **Skill:** Understanding and using vocabulary; recognizing sentence structure.

COMPREHENSION

up

up up

Girls jump up!

Directions: Have your child identify the word at the top of the page, then trace and write the words and sentences. Point out the use of capital letters and exclamation points in the sentences.
Skill: Understanding and using vocabulary; recognizing sentence structure.

ALPHABETICAL ORDER

A

C

B

Z

X

E

D

L

Y

K J

T

M

S

I

W

U

V

R

H

Q

F

P

N

G

O

Directions: Have your child connect the dots in alphabetical order from A to Z to form a picture. ***Skill:*** Recognizing alphabetical order.

VOWELS: SHORT O

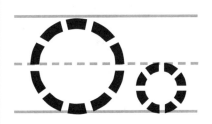  

top

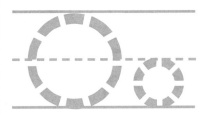   

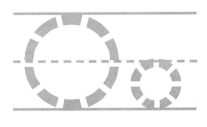   

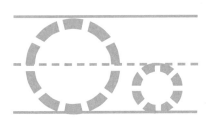   

Directions: Have your child trace Oo at the beginning of each row. Ask your child to say the word *top* while listening for the short o sound. Have your child name the pictures, then circle those that have the same short o sound as the picture at the top of the page. **Skill:** Identifying the short o vowel sound; writing Oo.

COMPREHENSION

The man rides __.

up   down

The girls jump __.

down   up

Girls __ a park.

fish   like

__ man rides up.

See   A

Directions: Have your child identify the pictures in each box, then circle the word that completes the sentence and describes the picture. **Skill:** Understanding and using vocabulary; recognizing sentence structure.

Answer Key

Top, Bottom

Left, Right

green

Matching

s	s	e	s	w
i	l	i	i	y
p	p	d	b	p
b	b	c	b	d
G	D	G	Q	G
N	N	R	N	M
Y	J	Y	P	Y
J	J	P	J	I

Numbers 1 to 10

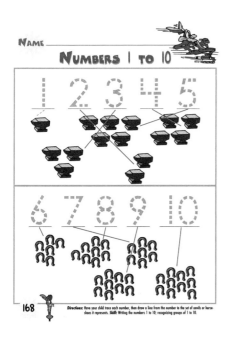

Beginning Sound K

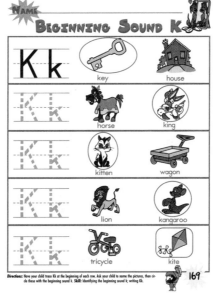

Kk key house
horse king
kitten wagon
lion kangaroo
tricycle kite

Comprehension

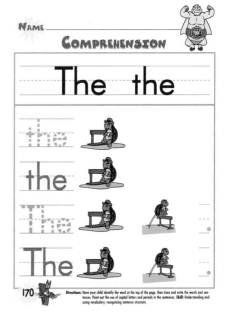

The   the

the

the

The

The

ANSWER KEY

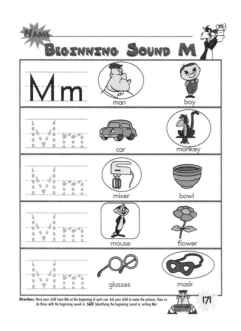

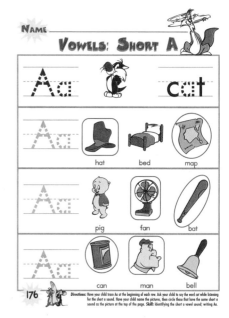

ANSWER KEY

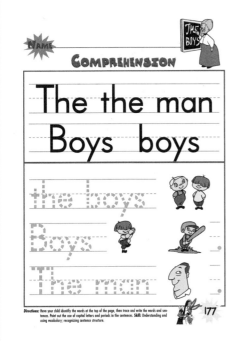

COMPREHENSION

The the man
Boys boys

Directions: Have your child identify the words at the top of the page, then trace and write the words and sentences. Point out the use of capital letters and periods in the sentences. Skill: Understanding and using vocabulary; recognizing sentence structure.

177

CLASSIFYING

178

Directions: Have your child identify the pictures, then circle those in each box that belong in the same category: the cat family, things to sit on, things to play with and things to ride. Skill: Identifying and classifying objects.

FIRST, MIDDLE, LAST

Directions: Have your child identify the pictures, then circle the last character in the first row, the middle character in the second row, the first train in the third row and the middle character in the fourth row. Skill: Identifying the positions first, middle and last.

179

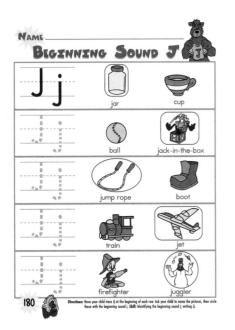

BEGINNING SOUND J

180

Directions: Have your child trace Jj at the beginning of each row. Ask your child to name the pictures, then circle those with the beginning sound j. Skill: Identifying the beginning sound j; writing Jj.

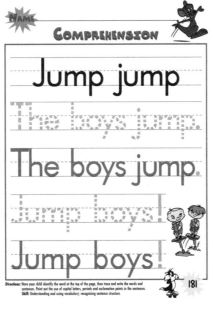

COMPREHENSION

Jump jump

The boys jump.

Jump boys!

Directions: Have your child identify the word at the top of the page, then trace and write the words and sentences. Point out the use of capital letters, periods and exclamation points in the sentences. Skill: Understanding and using vocabulary; recognizing sentence structure.

181

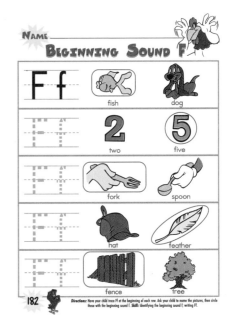

BEGINNING SOUND F

182

Directions: Have your child trace Ff at the beginning of each row. Ask your child to name the pictures, then circle those with the beginning sound f. Skill: Identifying the beginning sound f; writing Ff.

ANSWER KEY

COMPREHENSION

fish

Boys fish.

Boys fish.

The boys fish.

The boys fish.

Directions: Have your child identify the word at the top of the page, then trace and write the words and sentences. Point out the use of capital letters and periods in the sentences. **Skill:** Understanding and using vocabulary; recognizing sentence structure.

183

BEGINNING SOUND G

G g	girl	dog
G g	car	grapes
G g	wagon	gas
G g	lion	goat
G g	guitar	piano

184 *Directions:* Have your child trace Gg at the beginning of each row. Ask your child to name the pictures, then circle those with the beginning sound g. **Skill:** Identifying the beginning sound g; writing Gg.

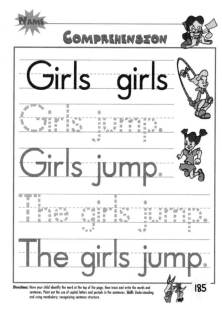

COMPREHENSION

Girls   girls

Girls jump.

Girls jump.

The girls jump.

The girls jump.

Directions: Have your child identify the word at the top of the page, then trace and write the words and sentences. Point out the use of capital letters and periods in the sentences. **Skill:** Understanding and using vocabulary; recognizing sentence structure.

185

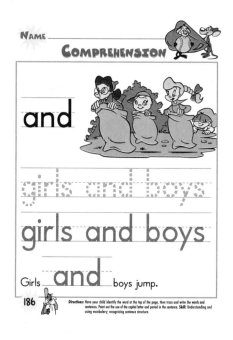

COMPREHENSION

and

girls and boys

girls and boys

Girls ___ and ___ boys jump.

186 *Directions:* Have your child identify the word at the top of the page, then trace and write the words and sentences. Point out the use of the capital letter and period in the sentence. **Skill:** Understanding and using vocabulary; recognizing sentence structure.

SEQUENCE

4	2
3	1
2	1
3	4

Directions: Ask your child to identify the pictures in each group, then number the pictures in the order in which they take place. **Skill:** Identifying a sequence of events.

187

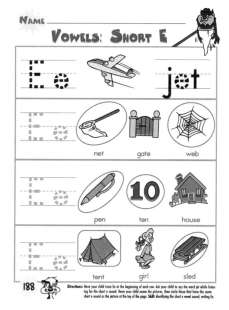

VOWELS: SHORT E

E e		jet
	net	gate	web
	pen	ten	house
	tent	girl	sled

188 *Directions:* Have your child trace Ee at the beginning of each row. Ask your child to say the word jet while listening for the short e sound. Have your child name the pictures, then circle those that have the same short e sound as the picture at the top of the page. **Skill:** Identifying the short e vowel sound; writing Ee.

230

ANSWER KEY

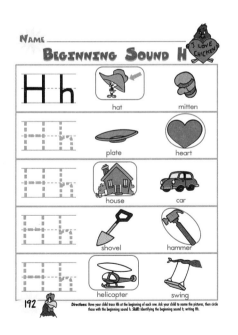

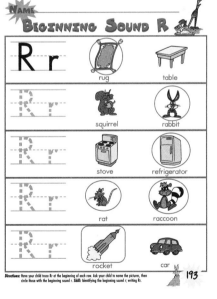

Answer Key

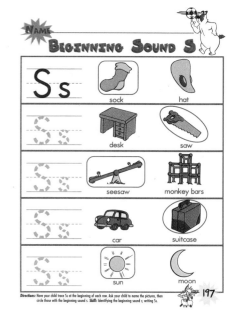

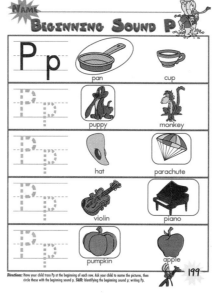

Answer Key

VOWELS: SHORT U

Uu — cup

bus — bed — duck

tree — sun — rug

nut — cow — drum

Directions: Have your child trace Uu at the beginning of each row. Ask your child to say the word cup while listening for the short u sound. Have your child name the pictures, then circle those that have the same short u sound as the picture at the top of the page. *Skill:* Identifying the short u vowel sound; writing Uu.

201

COMPREHENSION

The man ___. (rides) boys

Jump ___! park (now)

See the ___. (park) fish

Now the boys ___. jump (see)

202

Directions: Have your child look at the pictures in each box, then circle the word that completes the sentence and describes the picture. *Skill:* Understanding and using vocabulary; recognizing sentence structure.

MATCHING

paintbrush — apple — doll — paint

cup — book — saucer — car

toothbrush — teeth — snow figure — bicycle

watering can — comb — plant — monkey

saw — hat — whistle — board

Directions: Have your child name the pictures, then circle the picture that is related to the picture at the beginning of each row. *Skill:* Identifying and matching pairs of pictures.

203

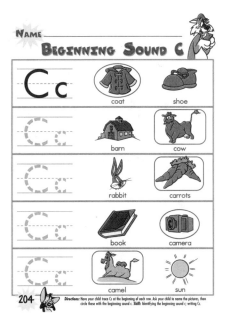

BEGINNING SOUND C

Cc — coat — shoe

barn — cow

rabbit — carrots

book — camera

camel — sun

204

Directions: Have your child trace Cc at the beginning of each row. Ask your child to name the pictures, then circle those with the beginning sound c. *Skill:* Identifying the beginning sound c; writing Cc.

COMPREHENSION

Can can

Can Can

can can

Can the man fish?

The man can fish.

Directions: Have your child identify the word at the top of the page. Ask your child to trace and write the words, then place them in the sentences at the bottom of the page. Point out the use of capital letters, the question mark and the period in the sentences. *Skill:* Understanding and using vocabulary; recognizing sentence structure.

205

BEGINNING SOUND Y

Yy — yarn — cat

jack-in-the-box — yo-yo

pencil — yardstick

yard — house

bed — yawn

206

Directions: Have your child trace Yy at the beginning of each row. Ask your child to name the pictures, then circle those with the beginning sound y. *Skill:* Identifying the beginning sound y; writing Yy.

233

ANSWER KEY

NAME

COMPREHENSION

You you

You can

You can

Can you ?

Can you ?

Directions: Have your child identify the word at the top of the page, then trace and write the words and sentences. Point out the use of capital letters, periods and question marks in the sentences. **Skill:** Understanding and using vocabulary; recognizing sentence structure.

207

NAME

BEGINNING SOUND T

T t

tie | shirt

knife | toaster

turtle | dog

toothbrush | cup

desk | typewriter

208

Directions: Have your child trace Tt at the beginning of each row. Ask your child to name the pictures, then circle those with the beginning sound t. **Skill:** Identifying the beginning sound t; writing Tt.

NAME

COMPREHENSION

to

to to to

to to to

Jump to the

Jump to the

Directions: Have your child identify the word at the top of the page, then trace and write the words and sentences. Point out the use of capital letters and periods in the sentences. **Skill:** Understanding and using vocabulary; recognizing sentence structure.

209

NAME

BEGINNING SOUND W

W w

wagon | car

flower | window

web | scissors

moon | waterfall

windmill | corn

210

Directions: Have your child trace Ww at the beginning of each row. Ask your child to name the pictures, then circle those with the beginning sound w. **Skill:** Identifying the beginning sound w; writing Ww.

NAME

BEGINNING SOUND Z

Z z

zipper | kitten

fish | zebra

zoo | bus

seven | zero

zigzag | paintbrush

211

Directions: Have your child trace Zz at the beginning of each row. Ask your child to name the pictures, then circle those with the beginning sound z. **Skill:** Identifying the beginning sound z; writing Zz.

NAME

COMPREHENSION

1

2

3

4

Answers will vary.

212

Directions: Have your child identify the pictures in each box and explain the sequence of events. Ask your child to draw a picture in the last box to show what happens next. **Skill:** Identifying a sequence of events; predicting an outcome.

ANSWER KEY

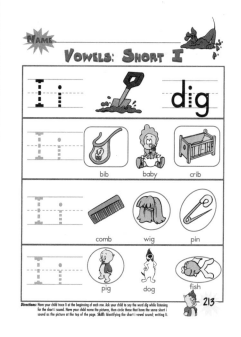

Vowels: Short I

Ii — dig

bib · baby · crib
comb · wig · pin
pig · dog · fish

213

Comprehension

The man rides __ a park.
(to) and

The man __ jump.
see (can)

Can __ jump?
(you) and

__ you see?
To (Can)

214

Directions: Have your child identify the pictures in each box, then circle the word that completes the sentence and describes the picture. Skill: Understanding and using vocabulary; recognizing sentence structure.

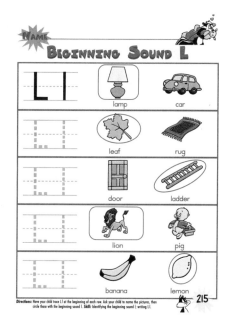

Beginning Sound L

L l

lamp · car
leaf · rug
door · ladder
lion · pig
banana · lemon

215

Directions: Have your child trace L l at the beginning of each row. Ask your child to name the pictures, then circle those with the beginning sound l. Skill: Identifying the beginning sound l; writing L l.

Comprehension

like

You like
You like
You like to
You like to

216

Directions: Have your child identify the word at the top of the page, then trace and write the words and sentences. Point out the use of capital letters and periods in the sentences. Skill: Understanding and using vocabulary; recognizing sentence structure.

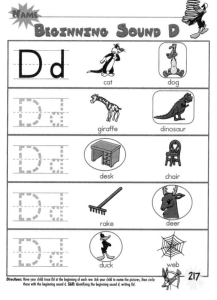

Beginning Sound D

D d

cat · dog
giraffe · dinosaur
desk · chair
rake · deer
duck · web

217

Directions: Have your child trace D d at the beginning of each row. Ask your child to name the pictures, then circle those with the beginning sound d. Skill: Identifying the beginning sound d; writing D d.

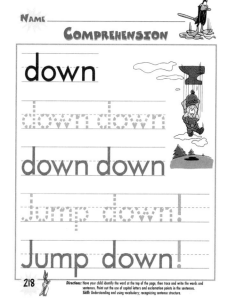

Comprehension

down

down down
down down
Jump down!
Jump down!

218

Directions: Have your child identify the word at the top of the page, then trace and write the words and sentences. Point out the use of capital letters and exclamation points in the sentences. Skill: Understanding and using vocabulary; recognizing sentence structure.

235

ANSWER KEY

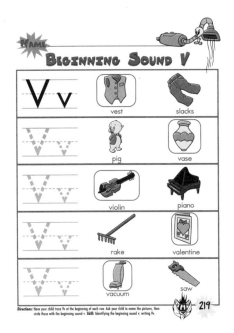

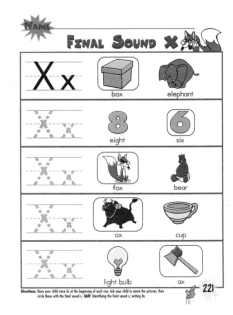

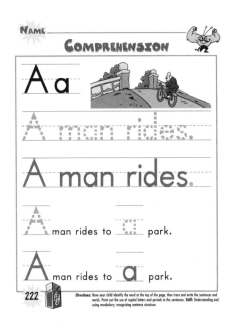

Answer Key

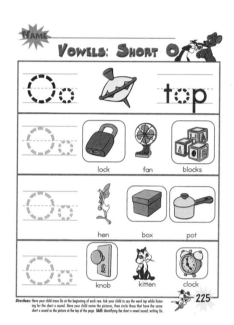

PRACTICE PAGE

Directions: Use this space to practice skills learned in the previous pages.

NAME

PRACTICE PAGE

Directions: Use this space to practice skills learned in the previous pages.

239

NAME

PRACTICE PAGE

Directions: Use this space to practice skills learned in the previous pages.

PRACTICE PAGE

Directions: Use this space to practice skills learned in the previous pages.

The Nation's #1 Educational Publisher

The **McGraw·Hill** *Companies*

Kindergarten

**Numbers & Counting • Addition
Subtraction • Money**

A McGraw·Hill/Warner Bros. Workbook

Table of Contents

Table of Contents (continued)

ONE AND TWO

Directions: Following the example in the first box, have your child draw scoops of ice cream on each cone to show how many. Then ask your child to color the cones with 1 scoop brown, and the cones with 2 scoops red. **Skill:** Identifying one and two.

WRITING 1 AND 2

1

2 2

Directions: Have your child trace, then write the numbers 1 and 2 in the space provided at the top of the page.
Then ask your child to count the mice in each block and write 1 or 2 to tell how many.
Skill: Identifying and writing 1 and 2.

NAME _____

THREE

1   2   ③

1   2   3

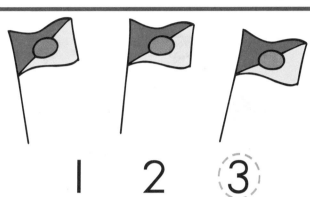

1   2   3

10,000 INSTANT MARTIANS Just Add Water

1   2   3

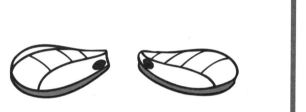

1   2   3

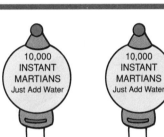 

1   2   3

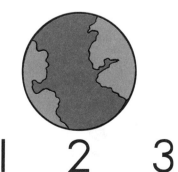

1   2   3

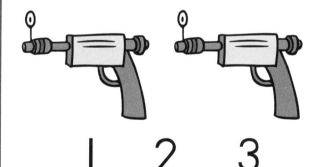

1   2   3

Directions: Have your child count the Martian objects in each block, then circle the correct number to show how many. **Skill:** Identifying groups of one to three.

NAME _____

FOUR

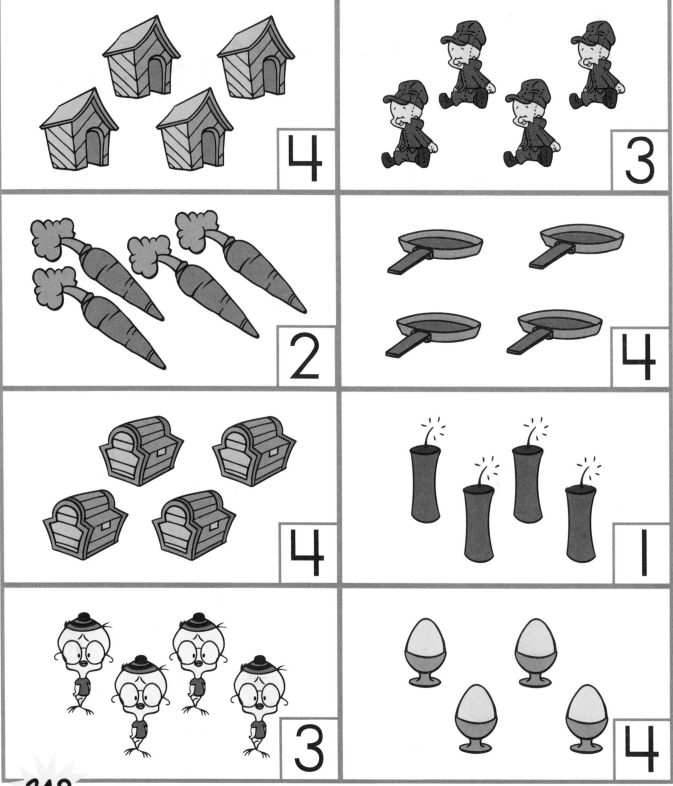

Directions: Have your child count the objects in each block, then circle the correct number to show how many.
Skill: Identifying groups of one to four.

WRITING 3 AND 4

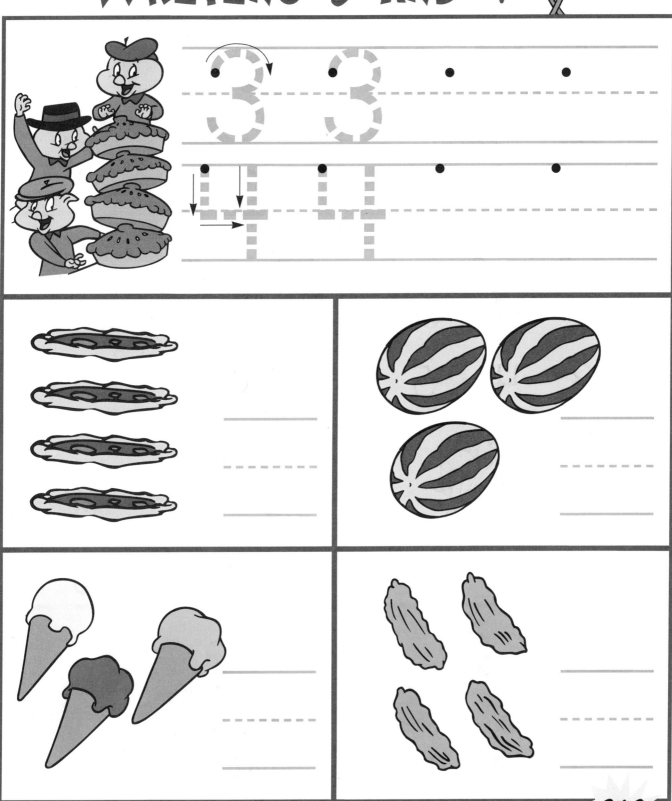

Directions: Have your child trace, then write the numbers 3 and 4 in the space provided at the top of the page. Then ask your child to count the food in each block and write 3 or 4 to tell how many.
Skill: Identifying and writing 3 and 4.

FIVE

3   4   (5)

2   3   4

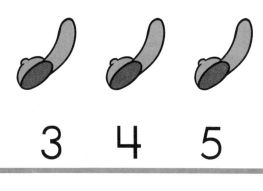

3   4   5

3   4   5

1   2   3

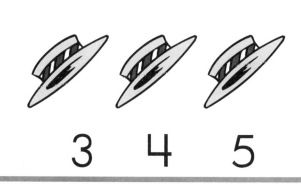

3   4   5

2   3   4

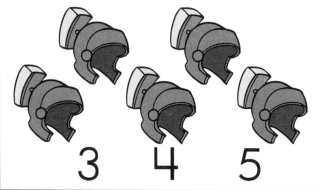

3   4   5

Directions: Have your child count the hats in each block, then circle the correct number to show how many.
Skill: Identifying groups of one to five.

ZERO

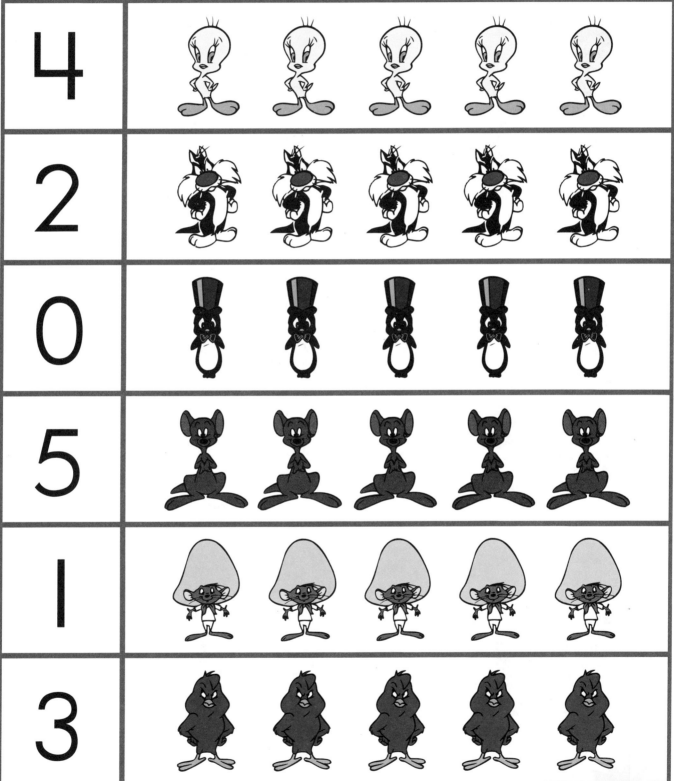

4	
2	
0	
5	
1	
3	

Directions: Have your child look at the numbers at the beginning of each row, then circle the correct number of animals to show how many. **Skill:** Identifying groups of zero to five.

NAME _____

WRITING 5 AND 0

252

Directions: Have your child count the birds in each block, then write 5 or 0 to tell how many. **Skill:** Identifying and writing 5 and 0.

NAME _____

ORDER 0 TO 5

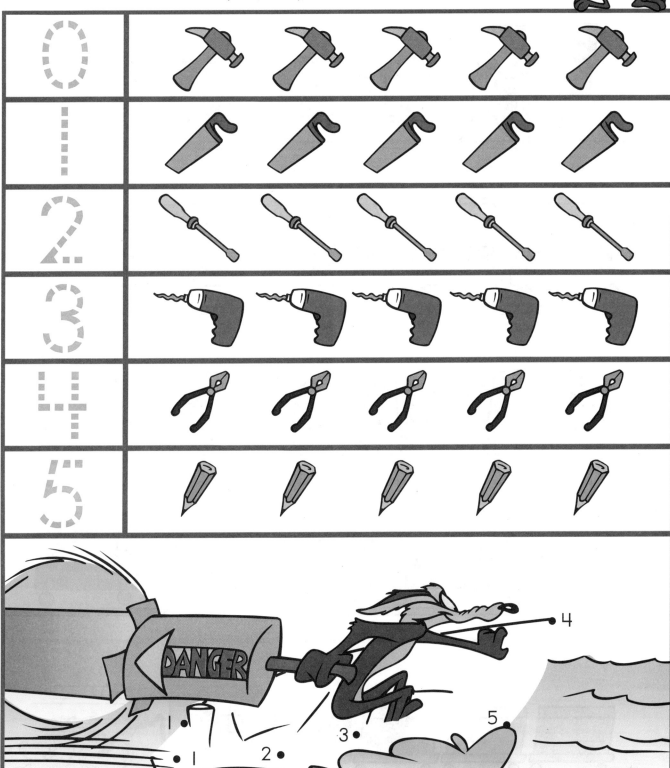

Directions: Have your child trace the numbers at the beginning of each row, then circle the correct number of tools to show how many. Ask your child to complete the dot-to-dot, starting at 0.

Skill: Identifying number order from 0 to 5.

ORDINALS TO FIFTH

Directions: Have your child circle the first car in the first row, the second car in the second row, and continue this pattern to the fifth row. **Skill:** Identifying ordinal positions first to fifth.

PROBLEM SOLVING

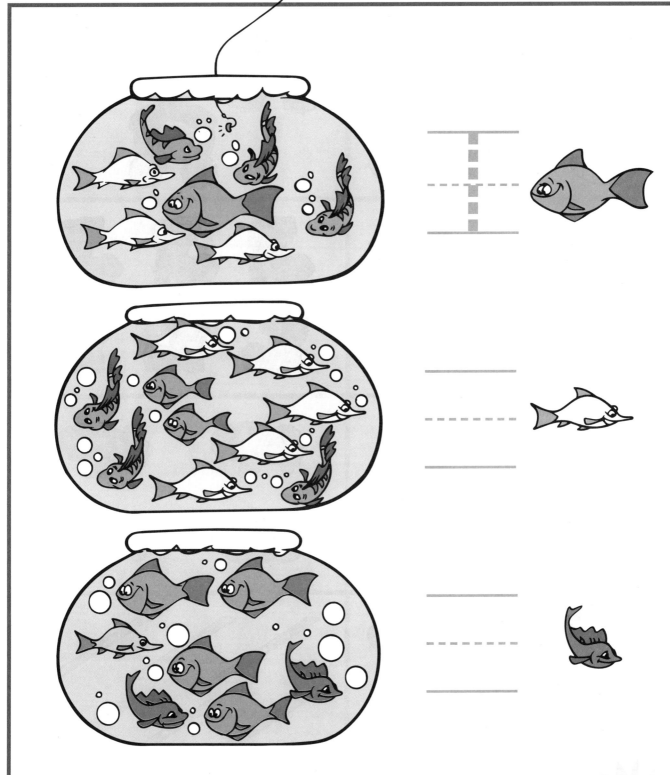

Directions: Have your child look at the fish on the right, then count how many of the same fish are in the bowl. Have your child write the number to show how many. **Skill:** Matching and counting.

SIX

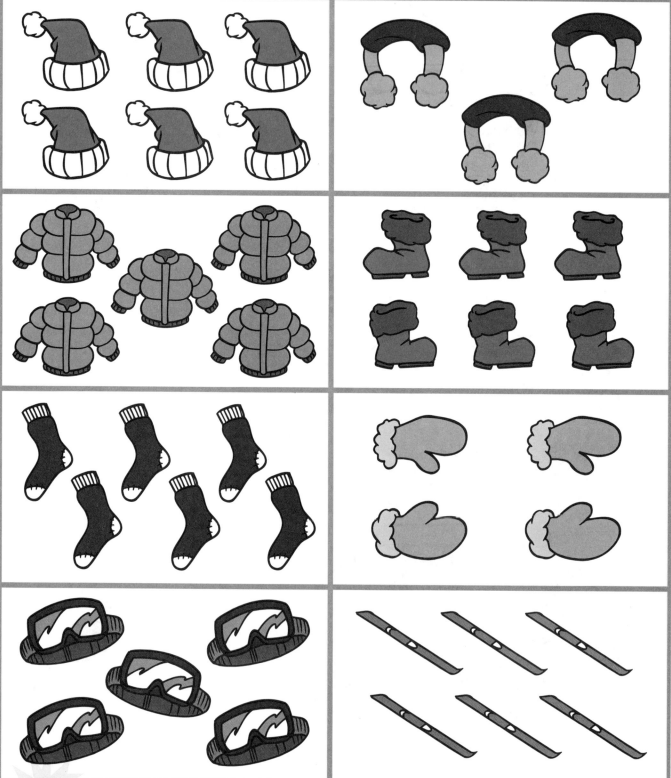

Directions: Have your child count the objects in each group, then circle the group if it shows 6. **Skill:** Identifying groups of six.

Seven

2   3   (4)

5   6   7

5   6   7

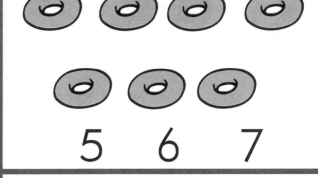

1   2   3

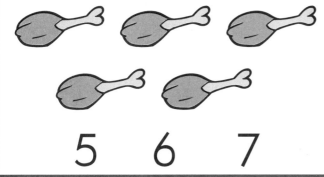

5   6   7

5   6   7

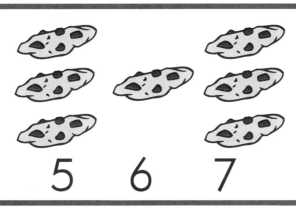

5   6   7

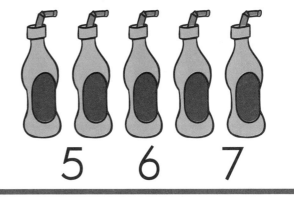

5   6   7

Directions: Have your child count the objects in each block, then circle the correct number to show how many.
Skill: Identifying groups of one to seven.

NAME _____

WRITING 6 AND 7

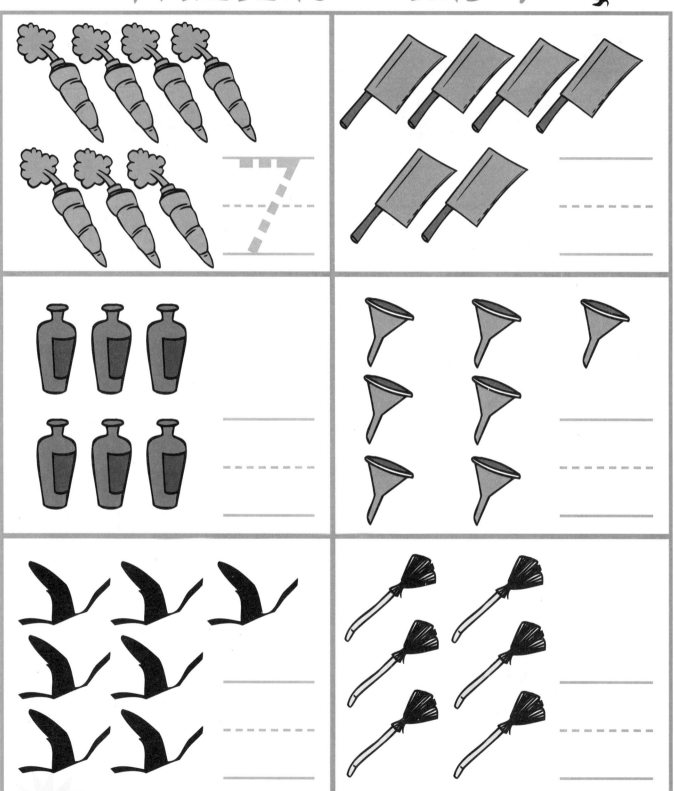

Directions: Have your child count the objects in each block, then write 6 or 7 to tell how many.
Skill: Identifying and writing 6 and 7.

EIGHT

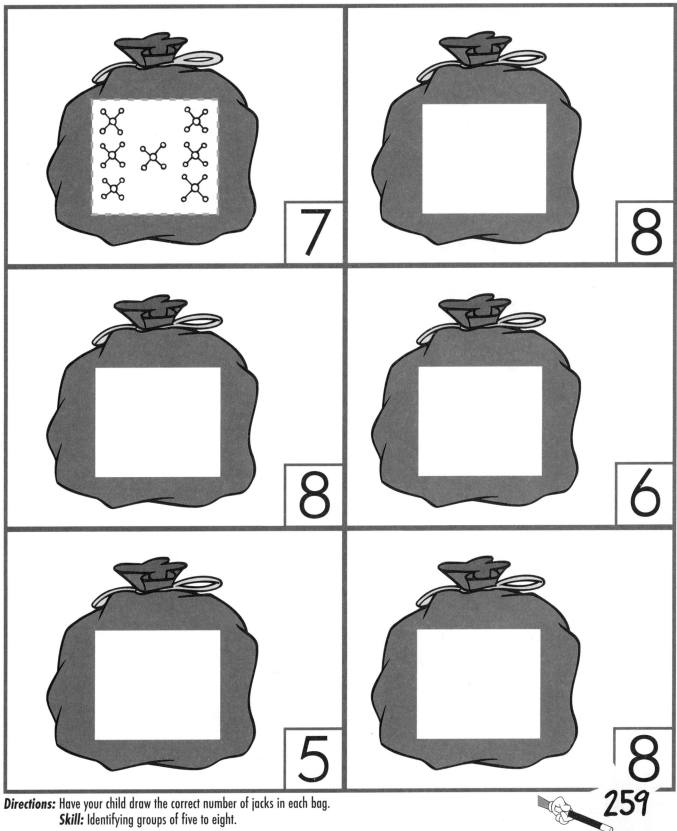

Directions: Have your child draw the correct number of jacks in each bag.
Skill: Identifying groups of five to eight.

259

NAME ____

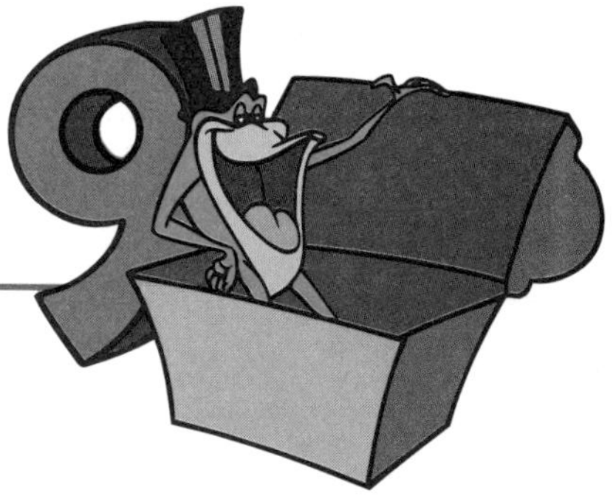

NINE

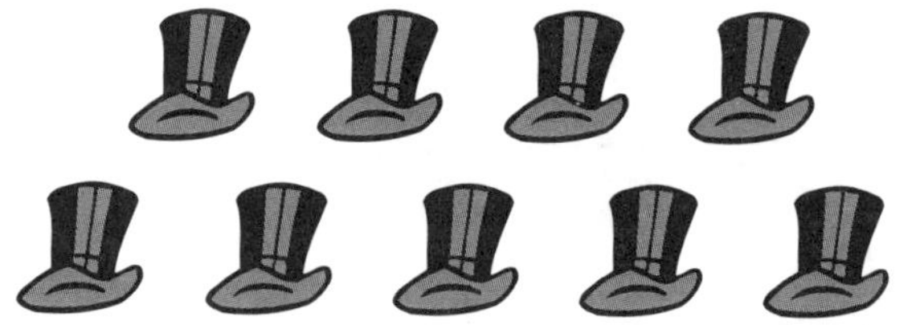

7 8 9

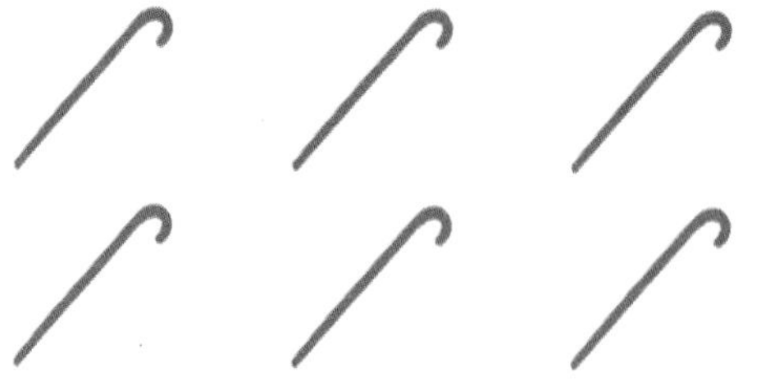

6 7 8

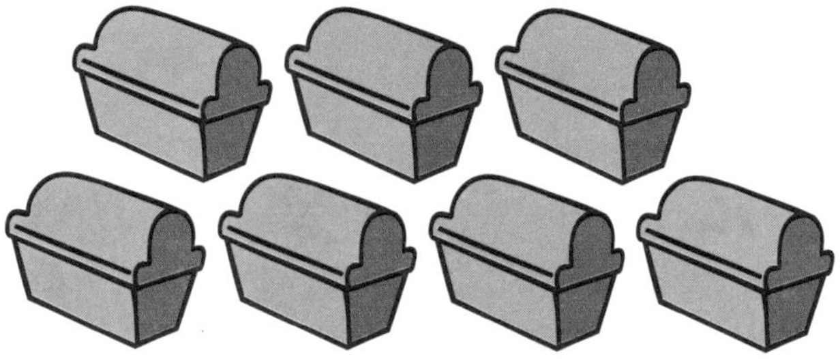

7 8 9

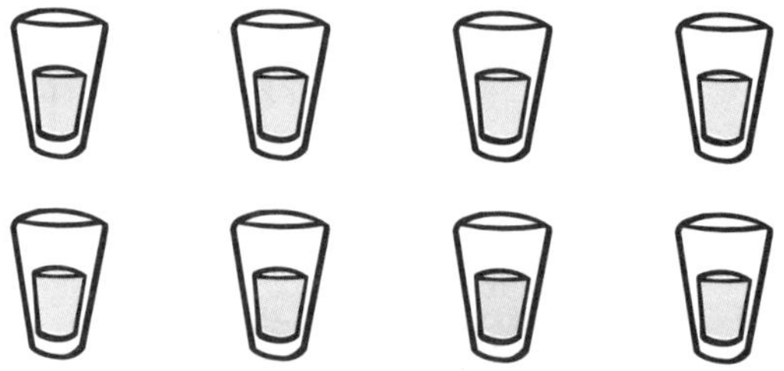

7 8 9

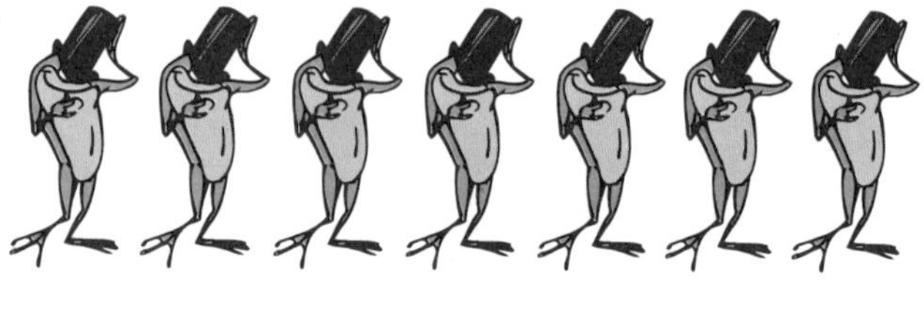

5 6 7

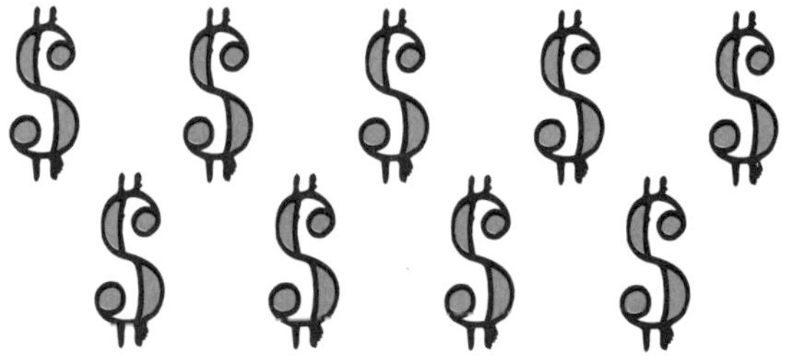

7 8 9

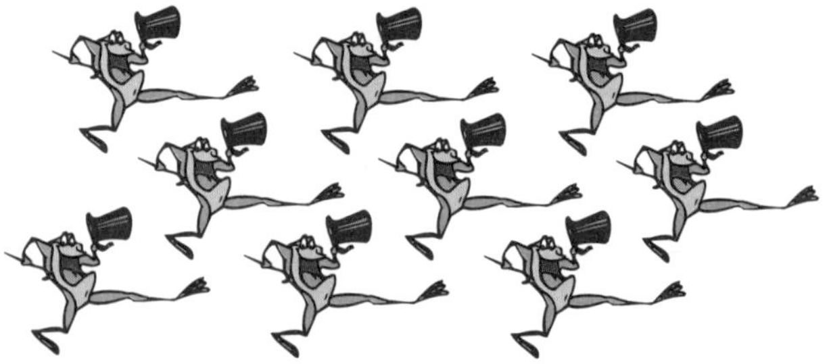

7 8 9

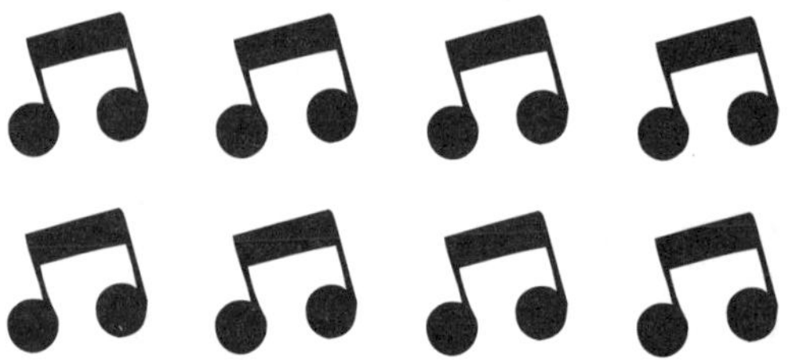

7 8 9

Directions: Have your child count the objects in each block, then circle the correct number to show how many.
Skill: Identifying groups of five to nine.

Writing 8 and 9

8

Directions: Have your child count the sports balls in each block, then write 8 or 9 to tell how many.
Skill: Identifying and writing 8 and 9.

Ten

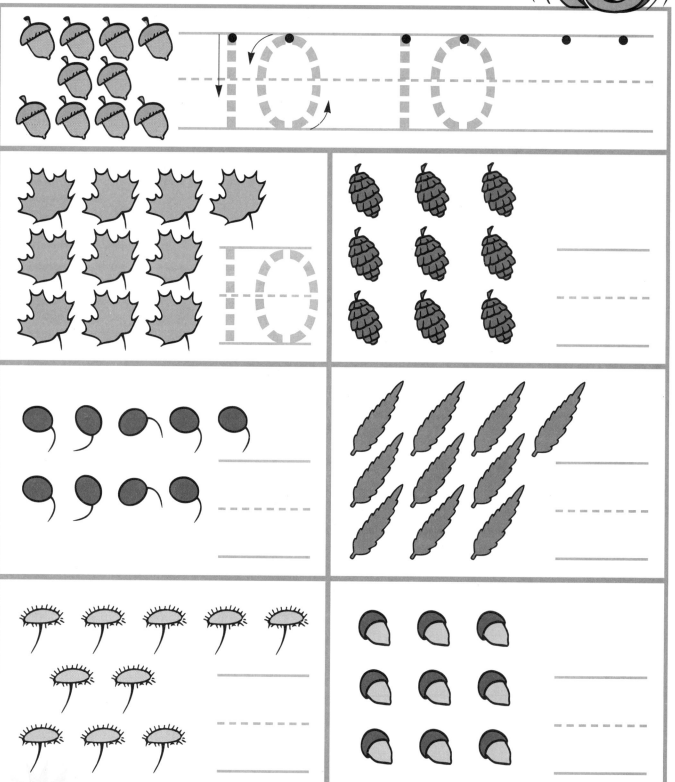

Directions: Have your child trace, then write the number 10 in the space provided at the top of the page. Ask your child to count the objects in each block, write the number to tell how many, then circle the groups that show 10. **Skill:** Identifying and writing 10.

ORDER 0 TO 10

Directions: Have your child count the holes in each poster and write the numbers in the space provided.
Skill: Identifying and writing 0 to 10.

263

MORE

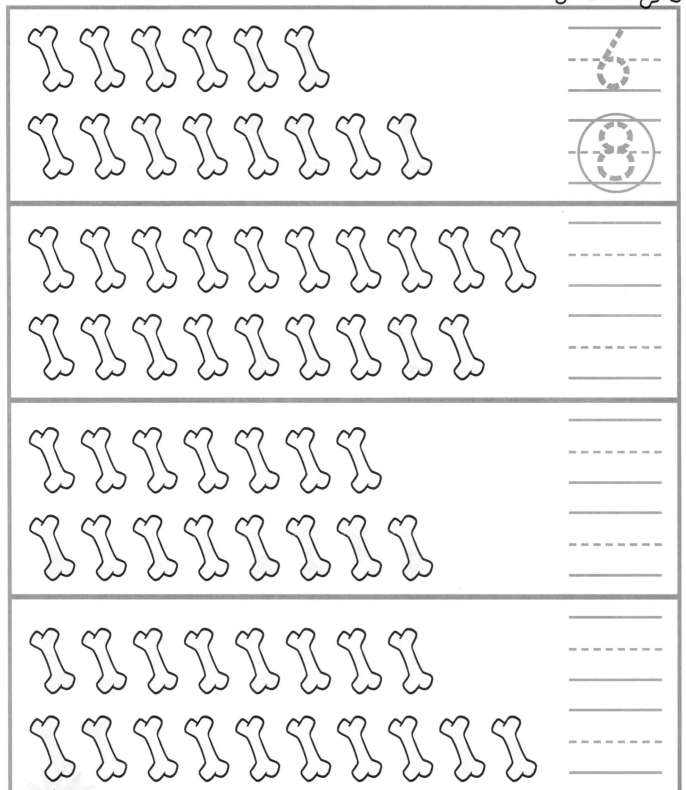

NAME

264

Directions: Have your child count the bones in each row, then write the number to tell how many. Ask your child to circle the number that is more. **Skill:** Counting to 10; identifying more.

Less

Directions: Have your child count the shoes in each row, then write the number to tell how many. Ask your child to circle the number that is less. **Skill:** Counting to 10; identifying less.

Eleven and Twelve

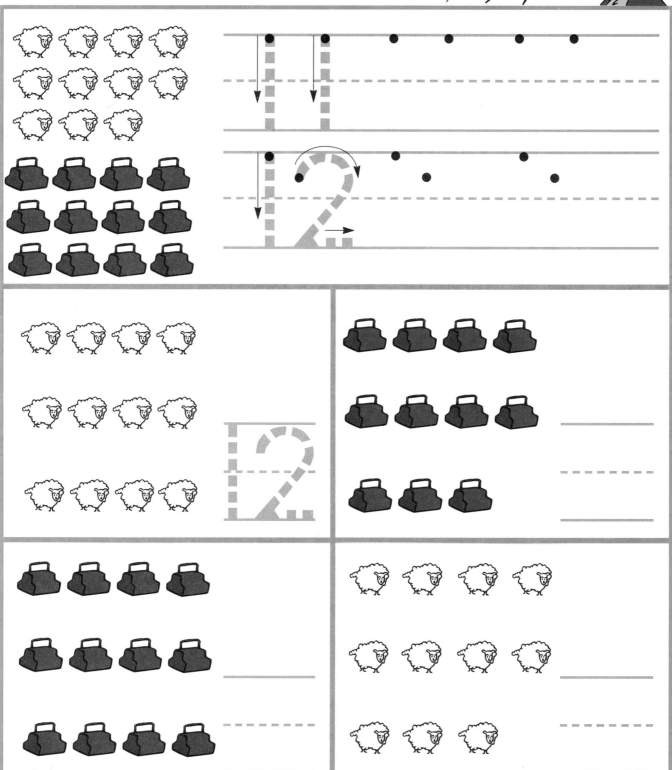

Directions: Have your child trace, then write, the numbers 11 and 12 in the space provided at the top of the page. Ask your child to count the lunchboxes and sheep in each block, then write 11 or 12 to tell how many. ***Skill:*** Identifying and writing 11 and 12.

GRAPHING

Directions: Have your child look at the graph and count the boxes for each animal. Ask your child to write the number that tells how many of each. **Skill:** Using a graph.

PROBLEM SOLVING

 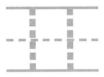 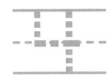 

0   1   2   3   4   5   6   7   8   9   10   11

Directions: Have your child look at the dogs, then read and trace the numbers under each. Ask your child to color that number of squares in the row next to each dog. **Skill:** Making a graph.

SHAPES

Directions: Have your child circle the objects that have the same shape as a box. **Skill:** Identifying objects of the same shape.

SHAPES

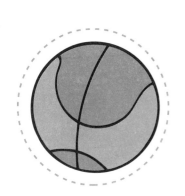   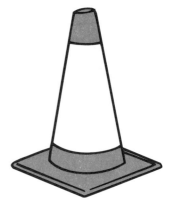

  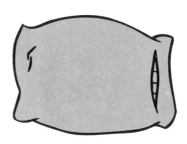 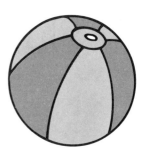

Directions: Have your child circle the objects that have the same shape as a ball. **Skill:** Identifying objects of the same shape.

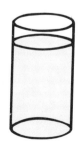

Directions: Have your child circle the objects that have the same shape as a can. **Skill:** Identifying objects of the same shape.

SHAPES REVIEW

 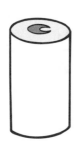  

   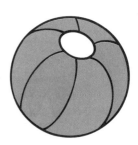

   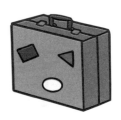

Directions: In each row, have your child draw an X on the picture that does not have the same shape as the other objects. **Skill:** Identifying objects of the same shape.

CIRCLE

 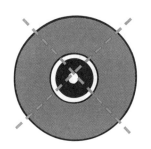  

  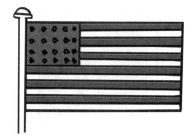

Directions: Have your child look at the pictures, then place an X on each object that has the shape of a circle.
Skill: Identifying a circle.

273

NAME

SQUARE

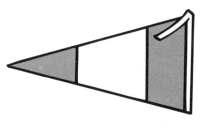

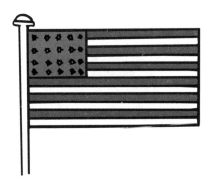
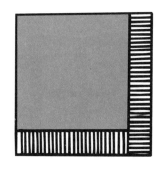

Directions: Have your child look at the pictures, then circle each object that has the shape of a square.
Skill: Identifying a square.

TRIANGLE

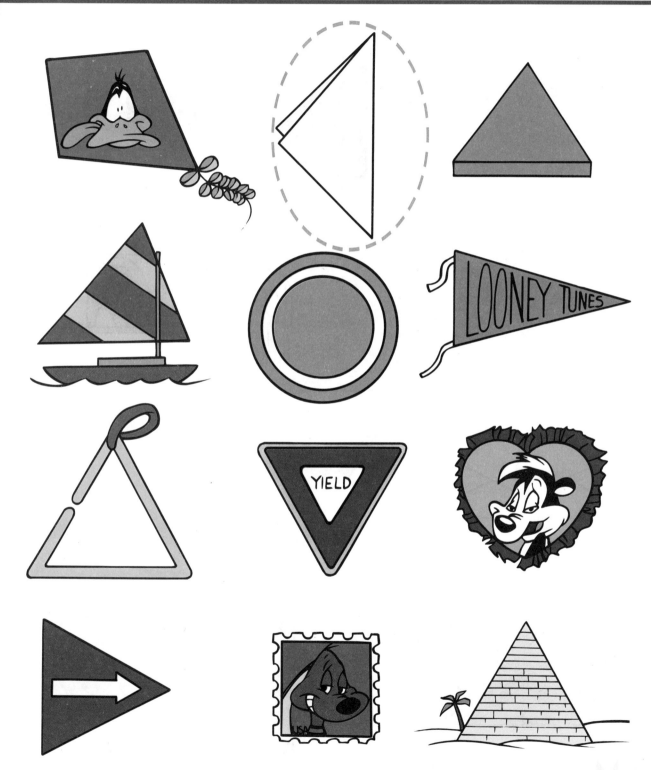

Directions: Have your child look at the pictures, then circle each object that has the shape of a triangle.
Skill: Identifying a triangle.

RECTANGLE

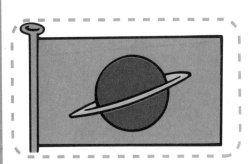

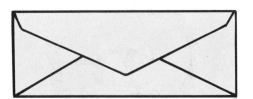

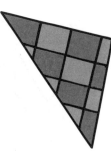

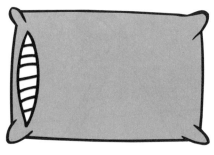

Directions: Have your child look at the pictures, then circle each object that has the shape of a rectangle.
Skill: Identifying a rectangle.

SAME SHAPES

Directions: Have your child color all squares red, all circles blue, all triangles yellow and all rectangles green. **Skill:** Identifying same shapes.

PATTERNS

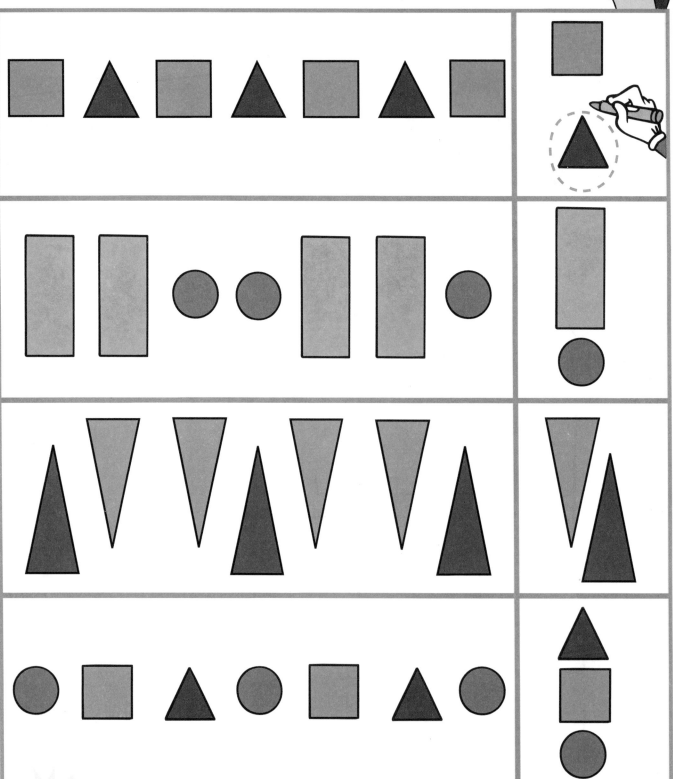

Directions: Have your child circle the shape that comes next in each row. **Skill:** Recognizing a pattern.

ONE HALF

Directions: Have your child look at each shape, then color one half if the shape has equal parts.
   Skill: Identifying one half.

PROBLEM SOLVING

Directions: Have your child match the faces by drawing a line from the picture on the left to the missing half on the right. **Skill:** Identifying one half; matching.

SEQUENCE

3   1   2

Directions: Have your child look at each picture and write 1, 2, and 3 to show the correct order of events.
    Skill: Identifying a sequence of events.

NAME

MORE TIME, LESS TIME

Directions: In each row, have your child look at each picture, then circle the one that takes more time and draw an X on the one that takes less time. **Skill:** Estimating time.

TIME

Directions: Have your child trace the dotted lines, then write the missing numbers. Ask your child to circle the number the short hand is pointing to. **Skill:** Recognizing a clock face.

 283

Penny

       5 ¢

       _____ ¢

     _____ ¢

    _____ ¢

      _____ ¢

284

Directions: Have your child count the pennies in each row, then write the number of how much money is shown.
Skill: Counting pennies.

NICKEL

Directions: Have your child circle the coin or group of coins that show 5 cents.
Skill: Identifying and counting pennies and nickels.

DIME

Directions: Have your child look at the price tag on the item at the beginning of each row. Ask your child to circle the coins needed to match each price tag. **Skill:** Counting pennies, nickels and dimes.

PROBLEM SOLVING

8¢

11¢

12¢

287

Directions: Have your child look at the price tags on the toys in the top row. Ask your child to draw an X on the coins needed to buy the toy. **Skill:** Counting money.

ONE MORE

288

Directions: Have your child color the white flowers purple, then write the number to show how many in all.
Skill: Counting and writing numbers.

ADDITION

2 + 1 =

3 + 2 = _____

3 + 1 = _____

2 + 2 = _____

Directions: Have your child count the dogs in each row, then write the number to show how many in all.
Skill: Adding objects.

ADDITION

$$3 + 2 = 5$$

$$4 + 1$$

$$3 + 1$$

$$4 + 2$$

$$1 + 2$$

$$2 + 2$$

Directions: Have your child count the squares in each row, then write the number to show how many in all.
Skill: Adding objects.

NAME

ONE LESS

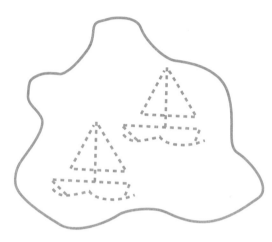

2

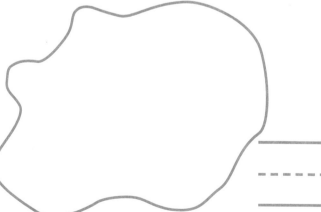

Directions: Have your child count the boats in each pond, then draw one less boat in the next pond. Ask your child to write the number to show how many boats were drawn. **Skill:** Identifying one less.

 NAME _____

SUBTRACTION

Directions: Have your child draw an X on the animals that are swimming away, then write the number to show how many are left. **Skill:** Subtracting objects.

293

SUBTRACTION

5 − 2 = 3

6 − 1 = _____

4 − 2 = _____

6 − 2 = _____

Directions: Have your child look at the bees in each row, then write the number to show how many are left.
Skill: Subtracting objects.

$$\begin{array}{r} 6 \\ -\ 2 \\ \hline 4 \end{array}$$

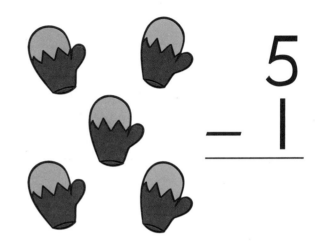

$$\begin{array}{r} 5 \\ -\ 1 \\ \hline \end{array}$$

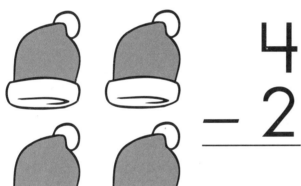

$$\begin{array}{r} 4 \\ -\ 2 \\ \hline \end{array}$$

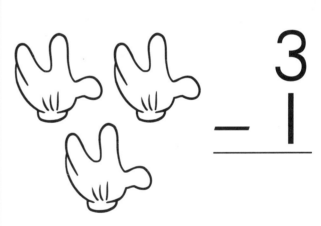

$$\begin{array}{r} 3 \\ -\ 1 \\ \hline \end{array}$$

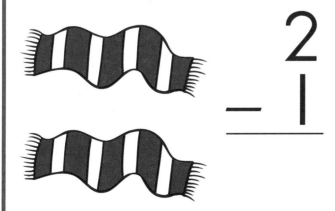

$$\begin{array}{r} 2 \\ -\ 1 \\ \hline \end{array}$$

$$\begin{array}{r} 5 \\ -\ 2 \\ \hline \end{array}$$

Directions: Have your child draw an X on the objects to show how many are taken away, then write the number to show how many are left. *Skill:* Subtracting objects.

295

PROBLEM SOLVING

$$5 - 3 = 2$$

$$3 - 1 = 2$$

$$2 + 4 = 6$$

$$4 + 1 = 5$$

$$4 - 1 = 3$$

$$5 - 1 = 4$$

$$2 + 2 = 4$$

$$2 + 1 = 3$$

Directions: Have your child circle the equation to match the picture. **Skill:** Recognizing addition and subtraction equations.

NUMBERS 0 TO 20

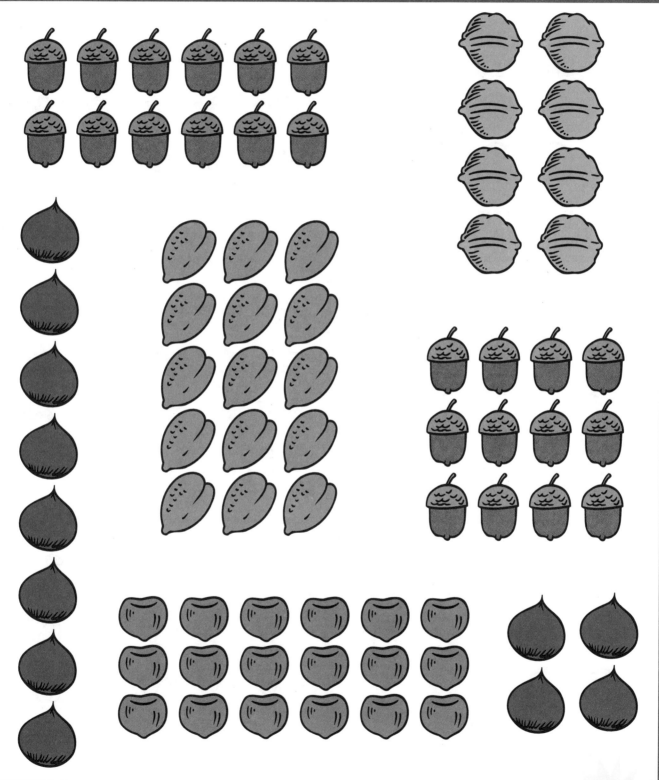

Directions: Have your child circle the groups that have more than 10 nuts.
    Skill: Counting to 20.

NUMBERS 13 TO 16

14   (15)   16

13   14   15

13   14   15

14   15   16

13   14   15

13   14   15

Directions: Have your child count the objects in each block, then circle the correct number to show how many.
Skill: Identifying groups of 13 to 16.

NUMBERS 17 TO 20

17

20

19

18

Directions: Have your child circle the objects to show the number at the beginning of each row.
   Skill: Identifying groups of 17 to 20.

NAME

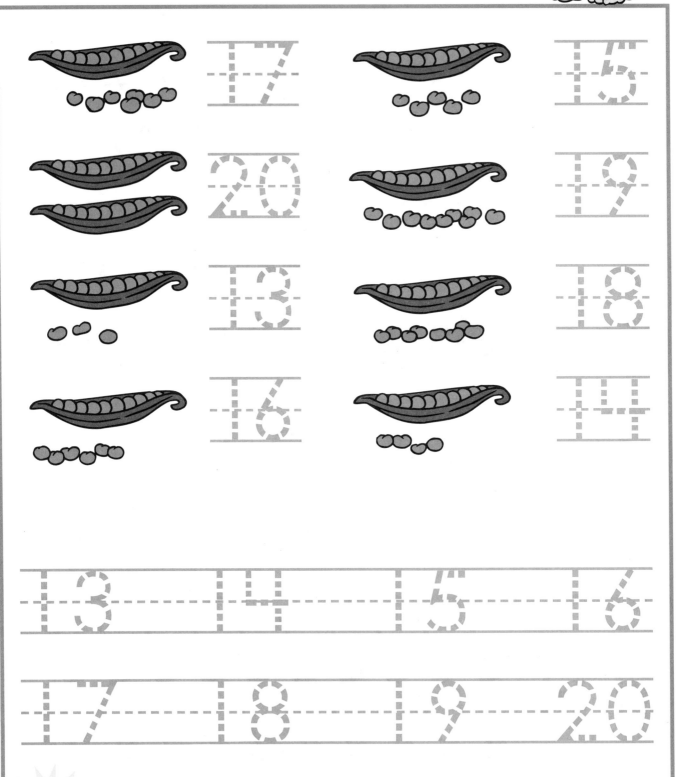

17

15

20

19

13

18

16

14

13   14   15   16

17   18   19   20

Directions: Have your child count the beans, then trace the number. At the bottom of the page, ask your child to trace the numbers in order. **Skill:** Counting and writing numbers to 20.

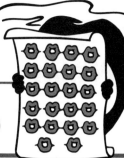

21

22

23

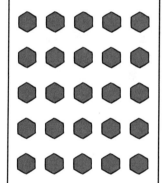

24

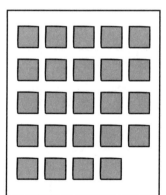

25

Directions: Have your child count each group of shapes, then draw a line to match each group to the correct number. **Skill:** Counting to 25.

NUMBERS 26 TO 30

27 (28) 29

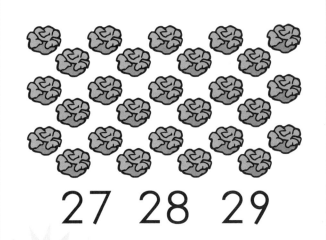

24 25 26

28 29 30

28 29 30

27 28 29

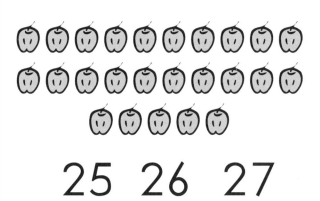

25 26 27

Directions: Have your child count the vegetables in each block, then circle the correct number to show how many. **Skill:** Identifying groups of 24 to 30.

CALENDAR

February

Sunday	Monday	Tuesday	Wednesday	Thursday	Friday	Saturday
	1	2				6
	15					
28						

Directions: Have your child trace the name of the month, then trace and write the missing numbers to complete the calendar. **Skill:** Reading a calendar.

PROBLEM SOLVING

21

23

27

14

Directions: Have your child look at the number in the left-hand corner of each picture. Ask your child to add 2 to the number, then write the new number. **Skill:** Adding and writing numbers.

WRITING NUMBERS 1 TO 15

1 2 3 4 5

6 7 8 9 10

11 12 13 14 15

Directions: Have your child practice writing the numbers in the spaces provided.
Skill: Writing the numbers 1 to 15.

WRITING
NUMBERS 16 TO 30

16   17   18   19   20

---

21   22   23   24   25

---

26   27   28   29   30

Directions: Have your child practice writing the numbers in the spaces provided. **Skills:** Writing the numbers 16 to 30.

ANSWER KEY

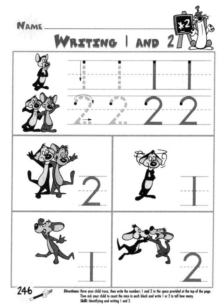

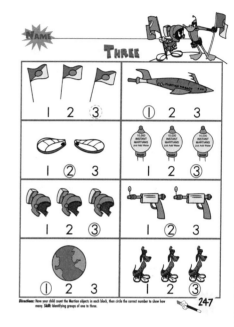

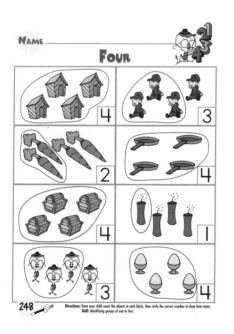

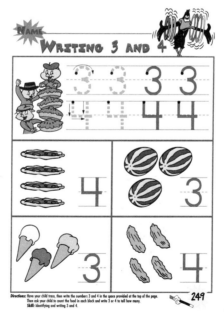

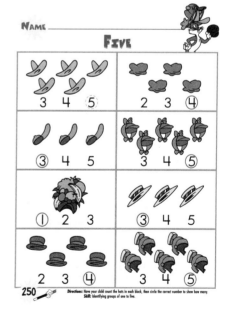

ANSWER KEY

ZERO

Directions: Have your child look at the numbers at the beginning of each row, then circle the correct number of animals to show how many. **Skill:** Identifying groups of zero to five.

251

WRITING 5 AND 0

252

Directions: Have your child count the birds in each block, then write 5 or 0 to tell how many. **Skill:** Identifying and writing 5 and 0.

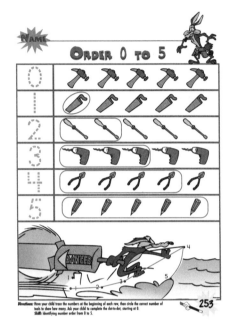

ORDER 0 TO 5

Directions: Have your child trace the numbers at the beginning of each row, then circle the correct number of tools to show how many. Ask your child to complete the dot-to-dot, starting at 0. **Skill:** Identifying number order from 0 to 5.

253

ORDINALS TO FIFTH

254

Directions: Have your child circle the first car in the first row, the second car in the second row, and continue this pattern to the fifth row. **Skill:** Identifying ordinal positions first to fifth.

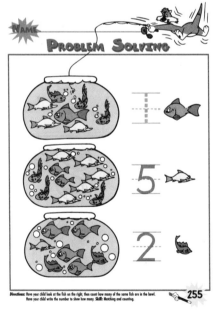

PROBLEM SOLVING

Directions: Have your child look at the fish on the right, then count how many of the same fish are in the bowl. Have your child write the number to show how many. **Skill:** Matching and counting.

255

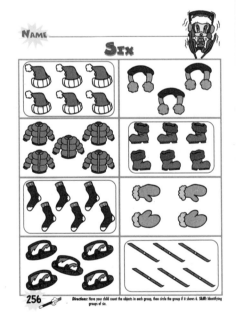

SIX

256

Directions: Have your child count the objects in each group, then circle the group if it shows 6. **Skill:** Identifying groups of six.

ANSWER KEY

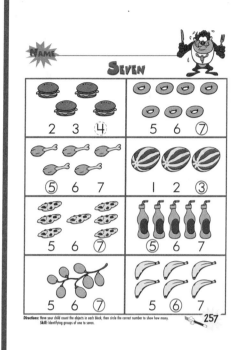

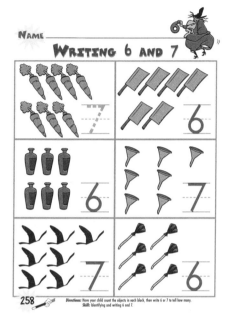

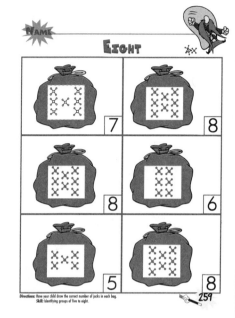

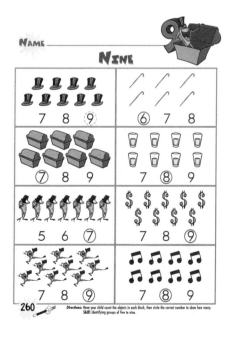

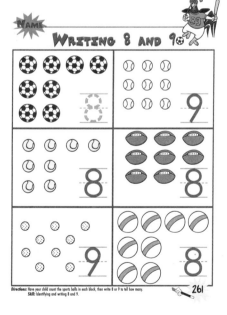

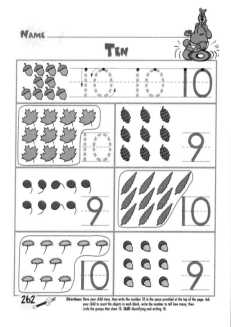

Answer Key

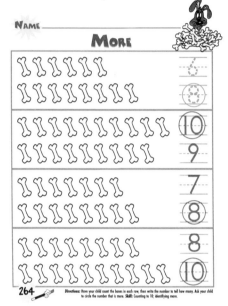

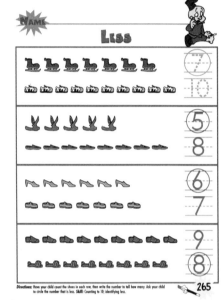

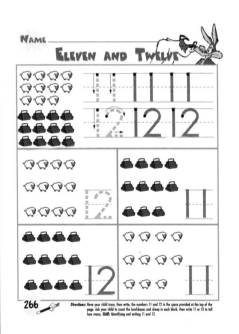

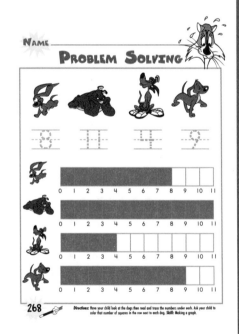

ANSWER KEY

269

270

271

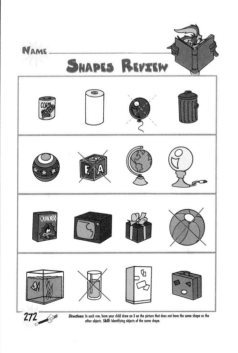

272

273

274

311

ANSWER KEY

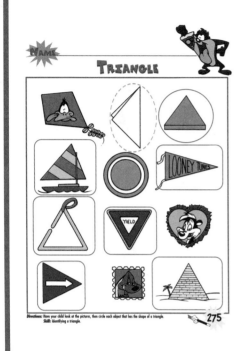

Directions: Have your child look at the pictures, then circle each object that has the shape of a triangle. Skill: Identifying a triangle.

275

276

Directions: Have your child look at the pictures, then circle each object that has the shape of a rectangle. Skill: Identifying a rectangle.

Directions: Have your child color all squares red, all circles blue, all triangles yellow and all rectangles green. Skill: Identifying same shapes.

277

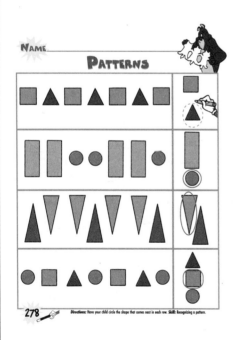

278

Directions: Have your child circle the shape that comes next in each row. Skill: Recognizing a pattern.

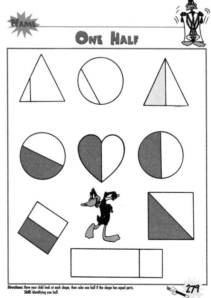

Directions: Have your child look at each shape, then color one half if the shape has equal parts. Skill: Identifying one half.

279

280

Directions: Have your child match the faces by drawing a line from the picture on the right to the missing half on the left. Skill: Identifying one half; matching.

Answer Key

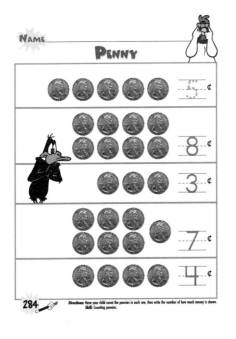

ANSWER KEY

PROBLEM SOLVING

Directions: Have your child look at the price tags on the toys in the top row. Ask your child to draw an X on the coins needed to buy the toy. *Skill:* Counting money.

287

ONE MORE

288

Directions: Have your child count the objects in each row, then draw one more. Ask your child to write the number to show how many in all. *Skill:* Counting and identifying one more.

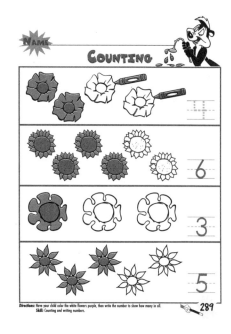

COUNTING

Directions: Have your child color the white flowers purple, then write the number to show how many in all. *Skill:* Counting and writing numbers.

289

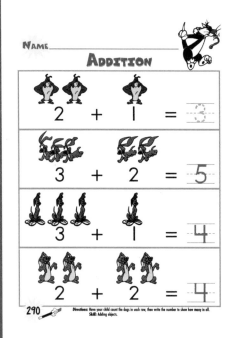

ADDITION

290

Directions: Have your child count the dogs in each row, then write the number to show how many in all. *Skill:* Adding objects.

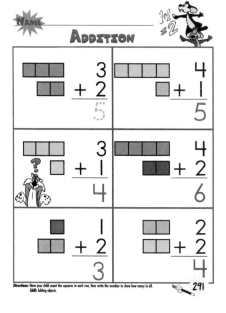

ADDITION

Directions: Have your child count the squares in each row, then write the number to show how many in all. *Skill:* Adding objects.

291

ONE LESS

292

Directions: Have your child count the boats in each pond, then draw one less boat in the next pond. Ask your child to write the number to show how many boats were drawn. *Skill:* Identifying one less.

ANSWER KEY

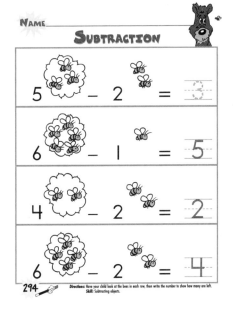

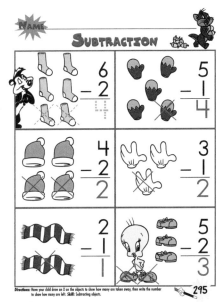

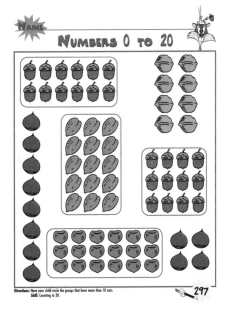

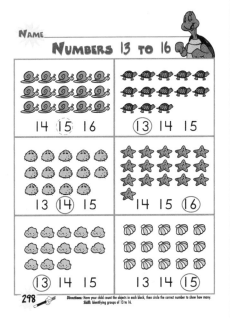

ANSWER KEY

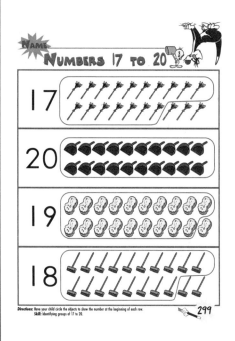

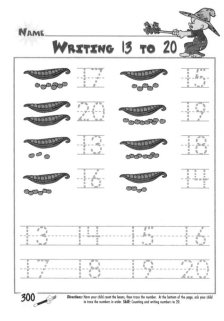

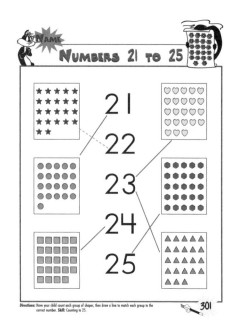

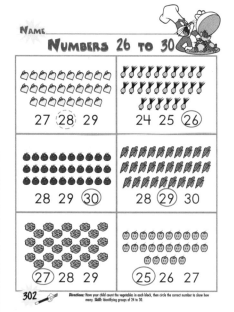

ANSWER KEY

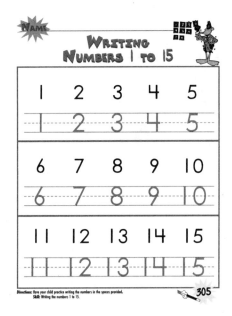

Name _____

WRITING
NUMBERS 1 TO 15

1	2	3	4	5
1	2	3	4	5

6	7	8	9	10
6	7	8	9	10

11	12	13	14	15
11	12	13	14	15

Directions: Have your child practice writing the numbers in the spaces provided.
Skill: Writing the numbers 1 to 15.

305

Name _____

WRITING
NUMBERS 16 TO 30

16	17	18	19	20
16	17	18	19	20

21	22	23	24	25
21	22	23	24	25

26	27	28	29	30
26	27	28	29	30

306

Directions: Have your child practice writing the numbers in the spaces provided. **Skill:** Writing the numbers 16 to 30.

CERTIFICATE OF ACCOMPLISHMENT

THIS CERTIFIES THAT

....

HAS SUCCESSFULLY COMPLETED
THE JUNIOR ACADEMIC'S™

Kindergarten Math

WORKBOOK.
CONGRATULATIONS AND THAT'S ALL FOLKS!

The **McGraw·Hill** *Companies*
....
PUBLISHER

Bugs Bunny
....
BUGS BUNNY, EDITOR-IN-CHIEF

RECEIVE THE McGRAW-HILL PARENT NEWSLETTER FREE!

Thank you for expressing interest in the successful education of your child. With the purchase of this workbook, we know that you are committed to your child's development and future success. We at *McGraw-Hill Learning Materials* would like to help you make a difference in the education of your child by offering a quarterly newsletter that provides current topics on education and activities that you and your child can work on together.

To receive a free copy of our newsletter, please provide us with the following information:

Name _____   Store where
                                          book purchased _____

Address _____   Grade _____

City _____ State ____ Zip _____ Title _____

e-mail (if applicable): _____

The information that you provide will not be given, rented, or sold to any company.

Mail to:
Parent Newsletter
c/o McGraw-Hill Learning Materials
P.O. Box 400
Hilliard, OH 43026-0400

This offer is limited to residents of the United States and Canada and is only in effect for as long as the newletter is published.